OCCASIONAL PAPERS SI

The *Parameters* of *Ḥalāl* and *Ḥarām* in Shariʿah and the *Ḥalāl* Industry

Mohammad Hashim Kamali

International Institute of
Advanced Islamic Studies (IAIS) Malaysia

THE INTERNATIONAL INSTITUTE
OF ISLAMIC THOUGHT
LONDON · WASHINGTON

THE INTERNATIONAL INSTITUTE OF ISLAMIC THOUGHT
P.O. BOX 669, HERNDON, VA 20172, USA
www.iiit.org

LONDON OFFICE
P.O. BOX 126, RICHMOND, SURREY TW9 2UD, UK
www.iiituk.com

P.O. BOX 12303, PEJABAT POS BESAR, 50774, KUALA LUMPUR, MALAYSIA
www.http://www.iais.org.my

ISBN 978-1-56564-555-4

Typesetting by Sideek Ali
Cover design by Shiraz Khan
Printed in Malta by Gutenberg Press Ltd

Series Editors
DR. ANAS S. AL-SHAIKH-ALI
SHIRAZ KHAN

CONTENTS

FOREWORD v

Introduction 1
Understanding the *Ḥalāl* and *Ḥarām* 2
The Permissible (*Ḥalāl*, also *Mubāḥ*, *Jā'iz*) 2
Ḥalāl and *Ṭayyib* Compared 6
The Principle of Original Cleanliness (*Ṭahārah*) 10
The Prohibited (*Ḥarām*) 14
The Grounds of *Ḥarām* 16
Ḥarām, Permanence and Change: The Principle of *Istiḥālah* (Substance Transformation) 18
The Reprehensible (*Makrūh*) 22
The Recommended (*Mandūb*) 26
The 'Grey Areas': Doubtful Matters 27
Food Enhancers and Additives 30
Mashbūh Ingredients and Additives 31
Ingredients and Additives that May Be Considered Unlawful 34
Requirements of a Valid Slaughter 35
The Role of Custom (*ʿUrf*) in the Determination of Values 38
Meat, Seafood and Dairy Products 40
The *Ḥalāl* Industry in Malaysia 41
Islam and Science 44
Conclusion and Recommendations 47

NOTES 51

FOREWORD

THE International Institute of Islamic Thought (IIIT) and the International Institute of Advanced Islamic Studies (IAIS) Malaysia have great pleasure in jointly presenting Occasional Paper 23 *The Parameters of Ḥalāl and Ḥarām in Shariʿah and the Ḥalāl Industry* by renowned scholar and specialist in Islamic Law and Jurisprudence, Mohammad Hashim Kamali. He has published widely on various Shariʿah topics. Many of his books including *Principles of Islamic Jurisprudence*; *Shariʿah Law: An Introduction*; and *A Textbook of Hadith Studies* are used as reference works in English speaking universities worldwide.

The subject of *ḥalāl* and *ḥarām*, notably meat, and meat products, is of central importance to Muslims with growing focus on ethical aspects of meat production, food safety and cleanliness, and the welfare of animals demanding greater attention. But there is more to the *ḥalāl* industry than simply meat. The issue of *ḥalāl* touches many areas of Muslim life. Because the industry is driven by the market realities of supply and demand, better understanding of Islamic principles is vital. The issue of additives for instance has caused considerable confusion in food consumption, just as the issue of banking interest has greatly baffled those seeking to invest ethically in order to avoid *ribā*. Not surprisingly, perceptions of what constitutes *ḥalāl* now vary among cultures and regions as well as followers of different schools of Islamic law. Exploring the question in detail, Kamali explains the basic principles of *ḥalāl* and *ḥarām*, referring to the Qur'an, and discusses key issues surrounding its implementation, giving important insights into the subject and cogently addressing many of the misconceptions confronting Muslims today. The work also offers practical advice for *ḥalāl* industry operators and seeks to advance uniformity in *ḥalāl* standards and proposes a set of guidelines to promote this.

Where dates are cited according to the Islamic calendar (hijrah) they are labelled AH. Otherwise they follow the Gregorian calendar and are labelled CE where necessary. Arabic words are italicised except for those which have entered common usage. Diacritical marks have been added only to those Arabic names not considered modern.

The IIIT, established in 1981, has served as a major center to facilitate serious scholarly efforts based on Islamic vision, values and principles. The Institute's programs of research, seminars and conferences during the last thirty years have resulted in the publication of more than four hundred titles in English and Arabic, many of which have been translated into other major languages.

Founded in 2008 in Kuala Lumpur, the International Institute of Advanced Islamic Studies (IAIS) Malaysia is an independent research institute, dedicated to objective academic research with practical policy-relevant implications on Islam and contemporary issues. In a relatively short period, IAIS has grown into a dynamic public forum that engages in seminars and publications of concern to Malaysia, the Muslim world, and Islam's engagement with other civilisations. IAIS Malaysia publishes a quarterly international peer-reviewed journal, *Islam and Civilisational Renewal* (ICR), a bi-monthly *IAIS Bulletin and Islam and Contemporary Issues*, books, monographs, and Occasional Paper Series. In the past five years it has convened about 150 events, seminars, roundtables, national and international conferences on a wide range of topics of concern to Islam and the Muslim world. Details on IAIS Malaysia activities and publications can be found at www.iais.org.my. Professor Kamali's own website is www.hashimkamali.com.

IIIT LONDON OFFICE *and* IAIS MALAYSIA, KUALA LUMPUR
August 2013

The Parameters of *Ḥalāl* and *Ḥarām* in Shariʿah and the *Ḥalāl* Industry*

INTRODUCTION

THE *ḥalāl* industry, although still in its early stages of development, has experienced remarkable growth. As a market phenomenon, the industry actually emerged in the first decade of 21st century. Its rapid progress is partly due to its stringent rules on food safety, cleanliness and economic fair play. As with Islamic banking in its early years, the *ḥalāl* industry has also been largely driven by market demands and realities. Market players and industry specialists now stress the need to enrich past achievements with efforts that advance a better understanding of Islamic principles and the scientific knowledge relevant to its future developments. This presentation begins with a review of evidence in the Qur'an, hadith and fiqh on the *ḥalāl* and *ḥarām*, beginning with an exposition of the basic rules of *ḥalāl*, and then proceeds to address the *ḥarām*, the reprehensible (*makrūh*) and the recommendable (*mandūb*) respectively. The discussion also explores the role that customary practice plays in the determination of these values, and the relationship also between Islam and science. Two other themes explored are the normative principle of cleanliness (*ṭahārah*), and the little known but important principle of substance transformation, or (*istiḥālah*), which explains the conversion of the *ḥarām* into *ḥalāl* due to internal chemical changes that removes the *ḥarām* element. A section of this presentation is also devoted to a review of the increasingly more relevant subject of the *mashbūhāt*, that is, doubtful matters that fall between the *ḥalāl* and *ḥarām*, which have not been regulated by the available evidence. Food additives, aspects of food processing and supply

---

* This article is an upgraded and enhanced version of a paper I presented at the World Halal Forum, Kuala Lumpur in May 2008.

chain, and doubts arising over the incessant stream of new food varieties that fall under the *mashbūhāt* are also discussed.

UNDERSTANDING THE *ḤALĀL* AND *ḤARĀM*

Muslim jurists have discussed the source evidence on *ḥalāl* and *ḥarām* and formulated guidelines to regulate their application to slaughter procedures and dietary substances. The Shariʿah identifies *ḥarām* substances in food and diet in specific detail, but takes a different approach to the identification of *ḥalāl* in foodstuffs and beverages as these are not always identified by name but by indicators that are not entirely free of doubt. Grey areas of doubt have consequently existed and often called for fresh juristic enquiry and ijtihad as to their permissibility or otherwise. The existing fiqh manuals provide details concerning almost every known variety of animals, birds, insects, seafood varieties and so on. Yet the unceasing diversity, in our times, of market products as well as new developments in science and technology continuously impact the fiqh positions on dietary substances, which necessitate, in turn, continuous research and review of the content and composition of food products from the Shariʿah perspective.

THE PERMISSIBLE (*ḤALĀL*, ALSO *MUBĀḤ*, *JĀ'IZ*)

Of the three Arabic words that appear in this heading, *ḥalāl* and its derivatives occur more frequently in the Qur'an and hadith, whereas the fiqh literature is more inclined to employ *mubāḥ* and *jā'iz*.[1] *Ḥalāl* may be defined as an act, object or conduct over which the individual has freedom of choice and its exercise does not carry either a reward or a punishment. *Ḥalāl* may have been identified by explicit evidence in the Shariʿah or by reference to the presumption of permissibility (*ibāḥah*) as explained below.

The scale of five values known to Islamic jurisprudence, namely the obligatory, recommendable, permissible, reprehensible, and forbidden (*wājib*, *mandūb*, *mubāḥ*, *makrūh* and *ḥarām*, respectively) does not occur in the Qur'an or hadith in that order. The Qur'an may use the word *ḥalāl* or its derivatives directly, or declare that 'there is no sin,' 'no liability,' 'no blame,' or that 'God will not take you to task' for such and such, all of which imply permissibility. This can also be said of the *makrūh* and the *mandūb*, for which a variety of expressions are employed in the Qur'an and hadith. Thus, when we read in these sources, expressions such as 'God does not love' such and such, or when an act is described as 'an abomination,' 'disliked,' 'misguided' and so forth, it would indicate a *makrūh*, and the opposite of such expressions may also imply a *mandūb*.[2]

The textual guidelines on *ḥalāl* suggest that no unnecessary restrictions should be imposed on the basic freedom of the individual and personal choice in what he or she wishes to consume, and the scope therefore of prohibitions should not go beyond what has been specifically determined by the text. The permissible, or *ḥalāl*, has consequently been left as an open category that applies to all that which is not forbidden. The Qur'an thus declares: "This day all things good and pure have been made lawful to you" (*al-Mā'idah*, 5:6); and "O mankind, eat of that which is lawful and wholesome in the earth" (*al-Baqarah*, 2:168 and 172); and then again: "O ye who believe! Forbid not the good things that Allah has made *ḥalāl* for you" (5:87). This outlook on *ḥalāl* has enabled the jurists to formulate general guidelines, such as the following legal maxim: "permissibility (*ibāḥah*) is the basic norm in all things unless there be evidence to establish a prohibition."[3] To declare something permissible one is not therefore required to produce supportive evidence for it beyond what may be obvious to the senses. Plant food and animal flesh is clean if general practice and reason indicate such and there is no obvious sign of impurity. No further Shariʿah proof is necessary. This basic permissibility subsumes what may be described as recommendable or reprehensible. For these basically consist of advice that may or may not be followed and the individual is not bound by them either. This is why the prominent Zahirite scholar, Ibn Ḥazm (d. 1064/456) has reduced the Five Scale of Values earlier mentioned to only three, namely the obligatory, the prohibited and the permissible, adding the point that recommended and reprehensible are basically the sub-varieties of permissible or *mubāḥ*.

Muslim jurists have also held that any textual evidence which overrules the presumption of permissibility must be decisive in both meaning and authenticity that is established by reliable reporting or transmission, simply because a *ḥarām* cannot be established on the basis of doubtful evidence, such as a weak hadith, or a Qur'anic verse that does not convey a clear meaning – in which case the subject would be governed by the presumption of permissibility.[4] The two main exceptions to *ibāḥah* Muslim jurists have noted are devotional matters (*ᶜibādāt*), and sexual intercourse between a man and a woman who are not married. The basic presumption here is that acts of devotion (*ᶜibādāt*) must be validated by a clear text, otherwise they are presumed to be forbidden, and that sexual intercourse between members of the opposite sex is generally prohibited unless there be a valid marriage. No one may thus add or detract anything from the five daily prayers, nor from the contents of each without the evidence of a clear text. For God Most High has determined the manner He is to be worshipped and we follow it as such.

The Mālikīs are the most liberal with regard to the permissibility of foodstuffs from animal sources that may have been classified under *makrūh* or even forbidden by the other schools. The Shāfiᶜīs, Ḥanafīs, and the Jaᶜfarī or Twelver Shiᶜites are moderate whereas the Ḥanbalīs tend to be restrictive. The Mālikīs permit all varieties of land and sea animals and birds, including the stray animals (*jallalah*) that feed on filth, and also birds of prey as well as ants, worms, and beetles to be permissible for human consumption. Most other schools have declared them as *makrūh* if not *ḥarām*.[5] This is in line with the generally more open and versatile chapter of Mālikī jurisprudence. It is the only school, or *madhhab*, for instance, that accepts the validity, in principle, of all the secondary proofs (*adillah farᶜiyyah*) of Islamic law known to all the leading schools of Islamic jurisprudence, whereas most other schools are selective in accepting some but rejecting others.

There are three types of *ḥalāl/mubāḥ*. First, *mubāḥ* that does not entail any harm to the individual whether he or she acts on it or not, such as travelling, hunting or walking in the fresh air. Second, *mubāḥ* whose commission is permitted due to necessity although it is essentially forbidden. This may include the consumption of carrion to save one's life.[6] The third variety of *mubāḥ* refers to conduct that Islam prohibited but which was committed before the advent of Islam or, with reference to converts, before they embraced the religion. For instance, wine-drinking was not prohibited until the Prophet's (ṢAAS)* migration to Madinah, hence it fell under *mubāḥ* until the revelation of the Qur'an verse which finally declared it forbidden (*al-Mā'idah*, 5:90).[7] Al-Ghazālī (d. 1111) has further explained that it is incorrect to apply *mubāḥ* to the acts of a child, an insane person, or an animal, nor would it be correct to call the acts of God *mubāḥ*. Acts and events that took place prior to the advent of Islam are not to be called *mubāḥ* either.

Mubāḥ has again been subdivided into three types:

1. Acts that are *mubāḥ* for the individual but recommendable (*mandūb*) for the community as a whole. Eating certain foods, such as vegetarian food, beef, mutton, and so on, is *mubāḥ* for the individual, but it is *mandūb* for the community as a whole to have them available in the marketplace.
2. Acts that are *mubāḥ* for the individual but obligatory (*wājib*) for the community as a whole. Under normal circumstances, eating, drinking and marriage may be *mubāḥ* for the individual, but to ensure their availability is a *wājib* for the community and its leadership. Similarly, it is *mubāḥ* for the individual to choose his line of work and profession, but the community as a whole is under obligation to ensure the survival of certain types of industries and trades.
3. Acts that are *mubāḥ* on an occasional basis but forbidden if pursued regularly. For example, an occasional use of harsh words on one's child is *mubāḥ* but forbidden if practised all the time, and *makrūh* if practised frequently.[8]

* (ṢAAS) – *Ṣallā Allāhu ʿalayhi wa sallam*: May the peace and blessings of God be upon him. Said whenever the name of the Prophet Muhammed is mentioned.

ḤALĀL AND *ṬAYYIB* COMPARED

Ṭayyib (lit. pure, clean) refers to objects, acts and conduct which are considered such by people of sound nature and people approve of it regardless of and independently of customary practices.[9] The opposite of *ṭayyib* (pl. *ṭayyibāt*) is that which is objectionable and repels people of good taste even if some people may find it otherwise.[10] As our earlier discussion of the grounds of *ḥarām* indicated, the basic relationship of *ḥalāl* and *ḥarām* with *ṭayyib* and *khabīth* is one of intrinsic and a natural inclination of *ṭayyib* to *ḥalāl* and of *khabīth* to *ḥarām*. Since God the Most High enacted the *ḥalāl* and *ḥarām* for people's welfare and benefit (*maṣlaḥah*), this becomes the basic cause and rationale behind the *ḥalāl* and *ḥarām*. He did not make anything *ḥalāl* without it being *ṭayyib* nor anything *ḥarām* which was not *khabīth*. When this natural relationship is disturbed, as it has been in some cases in the Qur'an itself, it has been for a specific reason.[11] *Ḥarām* in Shariᶜah is thus grounded in either natural repulsiveness (*khubth*) or harm and prejudice (*ḍarar*) or the two together. Broadly, whatever is purely or predominantly harmful is also *ḥarām*, and all that is purely or predominantly beneficial is also *ḥalāl*.[12]

Ṭayyib is not, however, a juridical category in that Islamic jurisprudence does not specify a separate value point by this name next to one might say that of permissible (*mubāḥ/ḥalāl*). The renowned scale of five values (known as *al-aḥkām al-khamsah*), as mentioned earlier, thus speaks of five values wherein *ṭayyib* is not featured as a separate category. Muslims are thus required to ensure that what they do, eat or drink is permissible in Shariᶜah, even if it is not pure, *ṭayyib*, or best quality. It would seem good enough for Muslims who live, for instance, in non-Muslim majority countries to observe the rules of *ḥalāl* without being asked to go a step beyond *ḥalāl* to that of *ṭayyib*. If someone chooses to be more particular and aim at what is *ṭayyib*, that is better of course. In some cases superior market facilities and supplies may even place Muslims residing in western countries in a better position to choose what is better quality and *ṭayyib*. As a juridical requirement, however, the rules of *ḥalāl* and *ḥarām* are what all Muslims need to consult and follow.

However, it may be said to be characteristic in many ways of all law in that legal rules tend to aim at the very high or the very low, as the case may be, of values pertaining to conduct - as compared to what people normally do in their daily lives. One may thus engage in deceitful activities and selfish pursuits, or eat unhealthy food or things which are merely permissible, but the law will not take one to task for it so long as the conduct in question does not amount to a crime or clear violation. This does not however mean that the Shariᶜah is not concerned with the higher reaches and objectives of personal conduct, which is why one also finds in the same scale of five values the category of recommendable, or *mandūb*. In the case of permissible/*ḥalāl* food, the law permits Muslims to eat certain things such as snails, worms, locusts, lizard, even crocodile and so forth, none of which can be said however to be *ṭayyib*. The distinction between *ḥalāl* and *ṭayyib* pertaining to victuals can relate more widely perhaps to Mālikī jurisprudence, which permits for eating a large variety of animals, birds, mammals and insects that are merely tolerated but evidently fall short of *ṭayyib*. *Ṭayyib* in the choice of food is all about purity and natural appeal, and thus belongs, for the most part, to the category of recommendable or *mandūb*, and not necessarily to that of *mubāḥ*.

It may be mentioned in passing that *ṭayyibāt* is not confined to food but extends, in the language of the Qur'an and hadith to other aspects of conduct, such as the line of work one does (cf., *al-Baqarah*, 2:267), just as it sometimes appears next to right ethical conduct (*al-Mu'minūn*, 23:51), the speech one utters (*al-Ḥajj*, 22:24), pure and upright individuals, men and women (*al-Nūr* 24:26) and even pleasant and comfortable residences (*masākin ṭayyibah*) (*al-Tawbah*, 9:72; *al-Ṣaff*, 61:12). *Ṭayyibāt* are often used as antonym to *khabā'ith*, be it in the edibles or what may relate to other aspects of conduct. *Ṭayyibāt* as such is a major theme of the Qur'an that encapsulates an exceedingly wide range of meanings. It is perhaps due to this factor that much of the Qur'anic usage of *ṭayyib* and its plural *ṭayyibāt* is understood to be a moral category which should be pursued and sought but that it may or may not constitute an obligation in itself.

To ascertain *ṭayyib* as a subset of *mandūb*, or even a category in its own right, in the context especially of victuals is even more meaningful in view of the so many new developments in food sciences, genetically modified food varieties, and mixing of additives and ingredients in the mass production of food. Factory production lines, commercially driven food processing methods tend to widen the scope of doubt in the natural goodness of food supplies in the marketplace. The *ḥalāl* food industry is thus well-advised to aim at *ṭayyib* as an optimal category of food that can eventually even be certified and labelled as such.

References to *ṭayyib* occur in numerous places in the Qur'an and hadith; in almost all places, however, *ḥalāl* and *ṭayyib* occur side by one another (*al-Baqarah*, 2: 167; *al-Mā'idah*, 5:4, 5:87; *al-Aʿrāf*, 7:157; *al-Nisā'*, 4:160). In other places, the Qur'an addresses the Prophet and the believers to "eat the *ṭayyibāt*" or "eat the *ṭayyibāt* from the sustenance We have provided you with." (*al-Mu'minūn*, 42, 51; *al-Baqarah*, 2:172). Reading them all together leaves little doubt that *ḥalāl* is also *ṭayyib* for the most part. This is the clear purport of the verse that reads in an address to the Prophet: "They ask you what is permissible (*uḥilla* - a derivative of *ḥalāl*) for them – say that which is *ṭayyib*" (*al-Mā'idah*, 5:4) but it is also typical of the Qur'anic reading to note that *ḥalāl* is mentioned first and *ṭayyib* after as if the text is conveying the message that *ṭayyib* is a step beyond and after *ḥalāl*.

According to a legal maxim of fiqh, "when the *ḥalāl* and *ḥarām* are mixed up, the *ḥarām* prevails".[13] In other words, when available evidence can imply both permissibility and prohibition, the latter prevails. While quoting this in his *al-Ashbāh wa al-Naẓā'ir*, al-Suyuṭī mentions that his maxim is based on a hadith to the same effect. The hadith thus provided "When there is a mixing of *ḥalāl* and *ḥarām*, the latter prevails." However, Muslim scholars including Abū al-Faḍl al-ʿIrāqī (d.806/1403), Tāj al-Dīn al-Subkī (d.1369/771) and Abū Bakr al-Bayhaqī (d.1064/456) considered this to be a weak hadith due to disruption in its chain of transmission.[14] Yet in circumstances where the amount of mixing and scope of confusion is slight to negligible, the legal maxim under review may also be of doubtful application. Some scholars have gone on record, moreover, to exonerate situations that involve minimal and sometimes unavoidable amounts of mixture with forbidden stuffs.

Confusion may also arise due to the existence of two divergent hadith reports, or two conflicting analogies: one prohibitive, and the other permissive, in which case the former prevails over the latter. Prohibition in this case takes priority over permissibility. This is the purport also of the legal maxim that "prevention of harm takes priority over realisation of benefit."[15] The doubt that arises over a text may be genuine (*ḥaqīqī*), such as ambiguity in the actual wording of a hadith, or it may be relative and metaphorical (*iḍāfī*, *majāzī*), and doubt arises in their application to a particular case. In all of these, an opportunity may arise for fresh interpretation and ijtihad, which should be attempted and an effort should be made to secure that which is in the public interest and *maṣlaḥah*. Thus in cases of confusion between lawfully slaughtered meat and carrion, the prohibitive position prevails and consumption is consequently not recommended. Similarly in the case of confusion arising between revenues from *ribā* and from a lawful sale, one should exercise caution on the side of avoidance. In the case of the hybrid breeding of animals, such as between a horse and a mule, most jurists would, however, take the mother's side as the stronger indicator of permissibility: If the mother is *ḥalāl*, the issue is also considered *ḥalāl*.

Should there be a mixture of two varieties of food, one *ḥalāl* and the other *ḥarām*, two situations may initially arise: Either the separation of the two parts is not feasible, such as when wine, blood or urine is mixed with water – then the *ḥarām* prevails over *ḥalāl*; or else the two parts can be separated, as when an insect or unclean substance falls on solidified butter – the object itself and its surrounding parts are removed and the rest becomes *ḥalāl*. However, if the mixture is of very small quantities that are hardly detectable and establishment of complete purity is not devoid of hardship, such as the remains of small amounts of alcohol in cooking utensils in big hotels, the doubt in them may be overlooked but avoidance is preferable.[16]

THE PRINCIPLE OF ORIGINAL CLEANLINESS (*ṬAHĀRAH*)

The principle of cleanliness (*ṭahārah*) is in many ways supplementary and parallel to that of permissibility or *ibāḥah*. A general position of note here is that whatever the Shariʿah has made *ḥalāl* is also pure and clean and all that which is made *ḥarām* is also most likely to be impure (*najas*). Original cleanliness also means that the normative position of Shariʿah with regard to all things is that of cleanliness.[17] It tells us that God Most High has created all things clean for the use and benefit of human beings unless there be evidence to suggest otherwise. Whereas the Mālikī school, has on the whole upheld an unqualified and general understanding of this principle, the Shāfiʿī and Ḥanbalī schools specify "all things" therein by saying that cleanliness is the norm with regard to all tangible objects (*al-aʿyān*) which include solid matter and animals, except for two: pigs and dogs. Dead carcasses are all unclean except for three: the human body (Muslim and non-Muslim alike), the fish and the locust. What is emitted from living animals, such as body fluids and sweat, also falls under the principle of original cleanliness, but according to an alternative view, only of the clean and 'slaughterable' (i.e. 'permitted') animals.[18] The Ḥanafīs are in agreement with the majority on this with one exception, which they make concerning dogs, by holding the view that dogs are not intrinsically unclean. The Mālikī's widen the scope further by holding that the Shariʿah presumption of cleanliness subsumes all things, including land and sea animals, dog and swine included. For life in itself is the effective cause (*ʿillah*) and criterion of cleanliness. What is prohibited is the flesh of these animals for consumption but they are not intrinsically unclean when alive. The body fluids of dogs and pigs, whether emitted in the state of wakefulness or sleep, except for the contents of their bellies, excrements and vomit, are also clean.[19] Cleanliness thus becomes an attribute of the created world and life forms therein. This is a corollary also of the basic Qur'anic position, which is one of specification concerning things that are unclean. Filth and impurities of things thus need to be determined by a clear text, failing which they are presumed to be clean. This limitation so expressed on the scope of *najas* and *ḥarām* is confirmed by the fact that the Qur'an specifies only ten items as *najas* for human consumption (cf., *al-Mā'idah*, 5: 3-4)[20] and then declares in an open address to the Prophet Muhammad: "They ask you what is made lawful for them. Say '(all) that is good and wholesome is made lawful'" (5:4). Thus it is not for us to expand the range of prohibitions, *ḥarām* and *najas*, beyond the textual specifications. Only a clear text, and failing that, factual evidence that makes dirt detectable by the senses, determines that something is impure/*najas*. Water is generally clean, for instance, for purposes of ablution, unless one detects dirt and impurity therein either physically or through the change of color and smell etc. In addition to text and palpable evidence, Muslim jurists have held that general consensus (*ijmāᶜ*) and inherited wisdom across the generations can determine what is unclean for human consumption. Thus only a clear text, factual evidence and general consensus can rebut and set aside the presumption of cleanliness.[21]

Arab linguistic usage and Islamic texts use a variety of expressions to signify defilement and dirt, whether inherent or putative, including *najas*, *qadhir*, *khabīth*, *rijs* and *rikz*. Fiqh scholars have divided the *najas* into two types, namely physical (*ᶜayniyyah*) and fictitious (*ḥukmiyyah*). Physical impurity is real and palpable to the senses and often inherent in the object itself. This is usually supported also by the Shariᶜah, which has in most cases identified inherently unclean substances. Physical dirt has been subdivided into three categories of intense, light, and average. If there is total consensus among juristic schools and scholars on the impurity of something, it is intense (*mughallaẓ*). Differences of opinion among them reduce the level to either average or light (*mutawassiᶜ* and *mukhaffaf* respectively). Without entering into details, these categories are often relevant also in determining the legality or otherwise of the sale and other uses of the items concerned. The basic position concerning *ḥarām* and *najas* is that, barring dire necessity, they may be neither consumed nor sold nor used for food, medicinal, cosmetic or other purposes, and that any contact with them is also likely to interfere with the integrity of one's ritual prayer (salah).[22]

Fictitious impurity is essentially a juridical attribute which may or may not be visible to the naked eye, but which the Shariʿah has identified as such, and it nullifies ablution for ritual prayer - for example, passing a motion, urination, or sexual intercourse. The state of cleanliness is restored either through taking a minor ablution (*wuḍū'*) or full bathing (*ghusl*) and washing generally with clean water. Other methods of purification of *najas* that the fiqh texts have recorded include drying and tanning, as in the case of animal skins, heating by fire and burning, pouring away certain quantities of water from a polluted water well, and ritual cleanliness through dry ablution (*al-tayammum*).[23]

The Shariʿah has also identified other varieties of impurity, such as the denial of faith (*kufr*), crime, and sin, which are deemed to pollute and compromise the purity of one's personality and character. This pollution may be removed by embracing the faith, or in the case of crime and sin, through prosecution and punishment, or through expiation (*kaffārah*) involving charity, fasting, and finally sincere repentance (*tawbah*).[24] As already mentioned, the consequence of declaring something as *najas* may be that this substance becomes wholly unlawful, even when mixed with other substances, for human consumption, or that it vitiates the ritual prayer when present on one's person, clothes, or the place of worship.[25]

The question as to precisely what items are *najas*, apart from the ones mentioned in the clear text is a subject of juristic disagreement. The first point of disagreement arises over the authority of determining the purity or impurity of objects, acts and conduct. Is it only the Shariʿah, or also popular custom and the natural predilections of people that can detect and determine legality and cleanliness? The fiqh scholars generally maintain that *najāsah* (filth) from the viewpoint of the Shariʿah is a particular category, which does not always correspond with what people may normally think. For example, the Shariʿah declares alcohol as unclean (*rijs*; cf., Qur'an *al-Mā'idah*, 5:90), a declaration which does not coincide with popular perceptions among the Arabs. Then also the Arabs consider certain things to be unclean which are not necessarily so in the Shariʿah. Included in these are certain human bodily emissions such as semen, spit, and mucus which are not textually declared to be unclean. People's perceptions thus vary according to their respective culture, climate and customary habits and do not always correspond with Shariʿah positions.[26]

Many fiqh scholars have drawn the conclusion that everything which the Shariʿah has made *ḥarām* is also *najas*. Yet a closer analysis would show that even this is likely to be less than accurate. For example, the Shariʿah prohibits marriage to one's mother or sister, which is *ḥarām* without question, yet the object of that prohibition, namely the women involved, cannot be said to be *najas* in themselves. In response, it has been stated that these prohibitions are not concerned with objects or persons as it were, but with relations, which are undoubtedly abhorrent but that there is no issue over inherent dirt and cleanliness of objects in this case. Yet the argument is further extended to other items such as poison, which may not be dirty as such but which the Shariʿah prohibits for consumption. Many scholars of the leading fiqh schools have also gone on record to say that even the birds and animals which the Shariʿah has prohibited for consumption, such as predatory animals and birds with claws and other characteristics, are not necessarily dirty in themselves, but that they have been declared prohibited for reasons most likely other than impurity (*najāsah*). This level of divergence is acknowledged in the fiqh maxim that "everything *najas* is *ḥarām*, but not all *ḥarām* is *najas*."[27]

The question still remains as to what exactly is the effective cause (*ʿillah*) of determining something as unclean/*najas*. If one could identify that the presence of a certain factor substance, or attribute means the presence of impurity/*najāsah*, and its absence also means that *najāsah* is absent, then one would have a formula and guideline to operate on. It is admitted, however, that we are unable to identify an effective cause or meaning of that kind. "Since this is a grey area and points of doubt still remain in the whole debate over *najāsah*, the *ʿulamā'* have held that we can only look at the textual injunctions of the Shariʿah to tell us what is *najas*. This is the only way and the best guideline to be applied."[28]

THE PROHIBITED (*ḤARĀM*)

Ḥarām (also known as *maḥẓūr*) may be defined as "all that which the Lawgiver (*al-Shāriᶜ*) has prohibited in definitive terms, and its perpetrator is liable to a punishment in this world or the Hereafter." *Ḥarām* may be an act, object, or conduct that is forbidden by clear evidence in the Qur'an or hadith. Committing *ḥarām* is punishable and omitting it is rewarded. This is the position of the majority of the legal schools of Islam (*madhāhib*). For *Ḥanafīs*, if the source evidence in question is anything less than definitive in respect of both authenticity and meaning, the *ḥarām* is downgraded to *makrūh taḥrīmī* (*makrūh* close to *ḥarām*) and no longer *ḥarām* in the full sense. The two resemble one another in that committing either is punishable and omitting rewarded, but they differ in so far as a wilful denial of the *ḥarām* incurs infidelity, which is not the case with regard to *makrūh taḥrīmī*.[29]

The Qur'an provides the primary proof in respect of *ḥarām*, as the text itself declares: "He (God) has explained to you in detail what is forbidden to you" (*al-Anᶜām*, 6:119), which means that a vague and inconclusive text is not enough to establish a *ḥarām*. With regard to prohibited food, for instance, the Qur'an has specified ten items, namely "carrion, blood, the flesh of swine, the animal slaughtered in any name other than Allah's, the animal which has either been strangled, killed by blows, has died of a fall, or by goring or devoured by a beast of prey...that which is sacrificed on stone (altars)," all of which are *ḥarām* (*al-Mā'idah*, 5:3).[30] The subject also occurs in two other verses which actually summarise the ten items into four (cf. *al-Anᶜām*, 6:145 and 2:172) as the last six items in the list of ten are actually included in the category of carrion. Wine drinking has also been declared forbidden (5:90). This is the sum total of clear prohibitions found in the Qur'an. As for the rest, it is ordained: "And do not utter falsehoods by letting your tongues declare: this is *ḥalāl* and that is *ḥarām*, thus fabricating lies against God" (*al-Naḥl*, 16:116). All other foodstuffs, animals of land and sea, harmful or unclean substances and so on, which are discussed in the fiqh manuals are subject to disagreement due mainly to the different perceptions of jurists concerning 'the grounds of *ḥarām*' as I elaborate below.

Although the hadith plays a role in determining what is *ḥarām*, the scope is fairly limited. This is the purport of the following hadith: Salmān al-Fārisī narrated that the Prophet was asked a question about the wild ass, quails and curdled milk, and he gave the following response: "*ḥalāl* is that which God has permitted in His Book, and *ḥarām* is that which God has prohibited in His Book. As for what He has chosen to remain silent about, it is exonerated."[31] Since there was no particular text in the Qur'an on the three items in question, they were consequently declared to be *ḥalāl*. Since the Prophet himself refers the determination of *ḥarām* mainly to the Qur'an there is little scope for anyone else, including the jurist, the *mujtahid* (one who exercises ijtihad), the mufti and the government authorities in the determination of *ḥarām*. Yet there is some flexibility for the head of state to prohibit what is a *makrūh* or make *mandūb* the subject of an obligatory command in order to realise a manifest *maṣlaḥah* (public interest), or prevent a manifest *mafsadah* (corruption, harm). This kind of discretionary power and its proper exercise is subsumed under the principle of Shariʿah-oriented policy (*siyāsah sharʿiyyah*) as explained below.[32]

Ḥarām is divided into two types: (a) *ḥarām* for its own sake (*ḥarām li dhātih*), such as theft and murder, carrion, blood shed forth, and so on, which are forbidden for their inherent enormity; and (b) *ḥarām* due to the presence of an extraneous factor (*ḥarām lighayrih*), such as a sale which is used as a disguise for securing usury (*ribā*). A consequence of this distinction is that *ḥarām* for its own sake is null and void (*bāṭil*) *ab initio*, whereas violation of a *ḥarām lighayrih* renders its subject matter into a *fāsid* (voidable) but not null and void, and a transaction over it may, according to the Ḥanafīs at least, fulfil some of its legal consequences. Most schools do not recognize *fāsid* as a separate category and would subsume the violations in question all under *bāṭil*. *Ḥarām* for its own sake does not become permissible save in cases of dire necessity (*ḍarūrah*), such as imminent death from starvation. *Ḥarām* due to extraneous factors becomes permissible in cases of manifest need and when it prevents hardship (*ḥaraj*).

According to a legal maxim of fiqh "the means toward *ḥarām* also partakes in *ḥarām*."[33] If theft and murder are *ḥarām*, the means toward procuring them are also *ḥarām*, and if pig meat is *ḥarām*, trading, processing, exporting and promoting it also partake in the same.

The rules of *ḥarām* are applied equally to all persons and places. It would thus be unacceptable, outside the situations of dire necessity, to make concessions in favour of particular individuals and groups, localities, climatic conditions and the like. Muslims may not relax the rules of *ḥarām* in their dealings with non-Muslims either, nor would it be valid to make concessions on the ground merely of common practice among people of something which is *ḥarām*.[34] Recourse to legal stratagems and ruses (*ḥiyal*) that seek to procure *ḥarām* under a different guise or name is also forbidden.[35] Good intentions do not justify the *ḥarām* either: in response to the question whether a *ḥarām* act can be combined with one that is intended to seek closeness (*qurbah*) to God – such as giving stolen food, or the proceeds of *ribā*, in charity – it is stated that the *ḥarām* overrides and suppresses the *qurbah*. An earlier noted, the *ḥalāl* and *ḥarām* are not always self-evident nor clearly identified in the sources, and grey areas persist between them which fall under the rubric of doubtful matters (*mashbūhāt*, also *al-shubuhāt*) that are separately addressed below. But before that, I propose to explore the grounds of *ḥarām* (*asbāb al-taḥrīm*), especially with reference to foodstuffs.

THE GROUNDS OF *ḤARĀM*

Muslim jurists have identified four grounds of *ḥarām* in foodstuffs: manifest harm, intoxication, filth/natural repulsiveness, and encroachment on the rights of others.

1. Manifest Harm (ḍarar)

Poisonous plants and flowers, snakes, scorpions, poisonous fish and arsenics are included in this category. Poison is forbidden for human consumption absolutely, according to the majority of the leading schools of Islamic law. However, the Mālikī and Ḥanbalī schools have held that some quantities of it may be used in medicine and treatment of disease.[36] This addition is generally agreeable as exceptional uses of poison are also covered under the subject of necessity (*ḍarūrah*). Harmful substances also include objects that may be harmful, even if not poisonous, such as eating mud, charcoal, harmful plants and animals etc. The Shāfiʿīs hold that these may not be *ḥarām* for someone who is not harmed by them, whereas the Ḥanbalīs classify these objects under the category of reprehensible (*makrūh*). Added to this is the proviso that identifying the harm in an object is not always self-evident and may need expert opinion.[37]

2. *Intoxication*

Intoxicants of all kind, including alcohol and all varieties of narcotics, whether liquid or solid are forbidden on the basis of clear textual mandates of the Qur'an (*al-Mā'idah*, 5:90), and the hadith which declares that "every intoxicant is like *khamr* [wine] and all *khamr* is *ḥarām*."[38] Since this is a *ḥarām* for its own sake (*ḥarām li-dhātih*), it is prohibited regardless of the quantity used, whether by itself or mixed with other substances and diluted, unless the mixture is such that it alters the nature of the substance and it no longer intoxicates – such as when wine turns into vinegar. Alcohol may not be used in medicine at first recourse, as per general agreement of the leading schools, although they all allow for situations of absolute necessity when, for example, it is known for certain that alcohol or its derivatives provide a cure to a disease and no other alternative can be found.[39]

3. *Filth, Impurity and Natural Revulsion (najas, rijs, khabā'ith, mustaqdharāt)*

These are either identified as carrion, spilt blood, pig meat (Qur'an, *al-Anʿām*, 6:145), or when people of sound nature and mind consider them as such. It may be solid, liquid, animate or inanimate. *Khabīth* (pl. *khabā'ith*, revolting, impure), being the antonym of *ṭayyib* (pure, clean) is a degree lower than both the *najas* and *rijs*. *Khabā'ith* accordingly subsumes predatory animals and birds as well as certain insects, such as lice and worms. They may not be *najas* in themselves, but they are subsumed, nevertheless, under the Qur'anic prohibition of *al-khabā'ith* (*al-Aʿrāf*, 7:157). Some substances are declared unclean because of the repulsion they invoke even if they are not filthy in themselves, such as human spit, mucous, sweat and semen, all of which are clean, but are declared non-*ḥalāl* for consumption on grounds of their natural repulsion.

4. *Unlawful Acquisition*

Forbidden foodstuffs and beverages also include unlawfully acquired property, such as stolen or usurped food and objects obtained through gambling, bribery, fraud and other unlawful means that are *ḥarām* under Shariʿah. This is the purport of the Qur'anic address to the believers to "devour not one another's properties wrongfully, unless it be through trading by your mutual consent" (*al-Nisā'*, 4:29).[40] An exception is granted in this connection to certain individuals, such as one's parent and guardian, the charitable endowment, or *waqf* administrator, and one compelled by dire need and threat of starvation.

ḤARĀM, PERMANENCE AND CHANGE: THE PRINCIPLE OF *ISTIḤĀLAH* (SUBSTANCE TRANSFORMATION)

Ḥalāl and *ḥarām* are basically permanent and unchangeable. What the Shariʿah has made *ḥarām* thus remains so for all time regardless of personal preferences, custom and culture. Shariʿah-rules on *ḥalāl* and *ḥarām* are also all-inclusive in that Muslims do not have the privilege of making something *ḥarām* for others and *ḥalāl* for themselves. These Shariʿah designations are meant to be for everyone, although certain exceptions have been made for non-Muslims, and even for Muslims themselves under stressful circumstances and danger to life. The renowned legal maxim of fiqh that "necessity makes the unlawful lawful – *al-ḍarūrāt tubīḥ al-maḥḍūrāt*,"[41] has wide applications to conditions of illness, advanced age, pregnancy, emergencies, and even travelling as a hardship category in its own right. Another basic position of the Shariʿah concerning *ḥalāl* and *ḥarām* to be noted is that small amounts and large all fall under the same rules. This is based on the authority of a hadith to the effect that when something is made *ḥarām*, even the smallest amount of it partakes in the same. Muslims are thus prohibited from consuming pork or alcohol, even a small quantity. The only exception taken by the Ḥanafī school that may be mentioned here is with regard to consumption of a very small quantity of liquor that does not intoxicate. In this instance the perpetrator is deemed to be guilty, yet not punishable with the prescribed punishment or *ḥadd* of wine drinking.[42] That said, however, any amount of consuming *ḥarām* becomes sinful even if it does not pollute or intoxicate, on grounds of caution and the Shariʿah principle of blocking the means to *ḥarām*, known as *sadd al-dharāʾiʿ*.[43] The leading schools of law have taken a similar position over taking of opium, other herbal intoxicants, and smoking of *ḥashīsh*, which are deemed harmful and thus fall under the ruling of the renowned hadith "*lā ḍarar wa lā ḍirār fī al-Islam* – harm must neither be inflicted nor reciprocated." Harm must, in other words, be avoided, whether it is inflicted on oneself or someone else. All intoxicants are harmful for human consumption Yet the perpetrator or one who consumes these additional substances is not held liable to the application of the *ḥadd* punishment of wine drinking. This is because of an element of uncertainty that obtains in the ruling of analogy (*qiyās*), which in this case has been drawn between wine and these other intoxicants. For the Qur'an only refers to wine but not to the other items mentioned – hence the uncertainty of extending the punishment of one to the other.[44] One may add, in passing that if fresh research and customary practice arrive at different positions based on stronger evidence, the fiqh rules may be accordingly adjusted. The *ḥarām* can, however, change into *ḥalāl* under certain circumstances that are expounded under the principle of *istiḥālah*.

Internal changes that alter the essence and basic properties of objects, such as chemical permutations occurring with or without human intervention, may alter the *ḥarām* and convert it to *ḥalāl* – such as the transformation of alcohol into vinegar, or when pig meat falls into salt and over time becomes an indistinguishable part of it. This transformation can occur naturally, as in the case of alcohol when an alcoholic substance is left in an open place or exposed to the sun, or when other substances such as onion, bread or yeast are immersed in it.[45] The fiqh principle that addresses changes of this nature is that of *istiḥālah*, or transformation, which is nowadays more frequently practised within the context of food augmentation or alteration due to chemical treatment and industrial intervention for trading, nutrition, medicinal and other purposes. According to the Islamic Organisation for Medicinal Sciences (IOMS), *istiḥālah* is the transformation of the natural characteristics of a forbidden substance to produce another substance with a different name, properties or characteristics. Substance transformation here refers to a chemical permutation, such as the process that changes oil and fat into soap or the decomposition of fats into fatty acids and glycerol through scientific intervention.[46]

Juristic opinion tends to differ over the legality and effects of *istiḥālah*. Can a Muslim consume or use an unclean substance if its chemical properties have changed? The majority opinion of the Ḥanafī, Mālikī, and Ḥanbalī, as well as the Shāfiʿī schools hold this to be permissible based on the reasoning that *ḥarām* exists due to unclean properties, and when they cease to obtain, the original status of permissibility is restored – as in the case of alcohol changing into vinegar. The rulings (*aḥkām*) of Shariʿah are founded in their proper and effective causes (*ʿilal*). When the effective cause of a ruling collapses and no longer obtains, its relevant ruling also collapses and should be replaced. The main exception to this is devotional practices (*ʿibādāt*) whose effective causes cannot be identified by the human intellect.

A different view is also recorded by a number of jurists within the leading schools holding that inherent impurity remains even after *istiḥālah* – as transformation is often partial and unclear. The majority view, however, has been adopted by the Ninth Fiqh-Medical Seminar (June 1997) of the International Organisation for Medical Sciences (IOMS), which held that additive compounds extracted from prohibited animals or defiled substances that have undergone *istiḥālah* are clean and permissible for consumption or medicine.[47] This is also the decision of the Islamic Fiqh Academy of the Muslim

League (held in Makkah, 13-17 December 2003) with the proviso that transformation is complete and that none of the original properties of the porcine substance is known to have survived. A partial transformation that causes only a change of form leaving the substance totally or partially unaffected, would thus fail to render the substance in question permissible.[48] Differences of opinion persist, however, over the usage of lard in food processing and also gelatin, both of which are porcine derivatives, although gelatin can also be obtained from other animals and, according to more recent research, from certain varieties of fish. A general advisory note is inserted, however, that one should try to avoid doubtful substances where other options are easily available and there is no compelling necessity otherwise.

The Eighth Fiqh-Medical Seminar of 1996, organised by IOMS, held that foodstuffs containing lard which does not undergo denaturation, such as in cheeses, vegetable oil, lubricants, cream, biscuits and ice cream, are prohibited due to the impermissibility of the pig and its derivatives. The same prohibitive stance is taken regarding ointments, creams and cosmetics which contain pig fat unless the substances from which they are derived undergo a transformation that eliminates their original properties.[49]

Gelatin derived from swine is used as a food ingredient for gelling, stabilising and emulsifying. Expert opinion has it, however, that gelatin whether from porcine, bovine or other animal sources undergoes transformation that fulfils the Islamic law requirements of *istiḥālah*, and as such is not prohibited. This is because gelatin no longer possesses the original attributes of the skin and bone of swine or carrion from which it was derived. Since it no longer has the same form, taste, smell or chemical structure of its original source, it falls under the basic norm of permissibility.[50] The Eighth Fiqh-Medical Seminar already referred to also held that "gelatin made of unclean animal's bones, skin and tendons is clean and permissible for consumption."[51] This may also be said of the water purification process attempted in countries facing water shortage. I read a news item some time ago with a picture of the then incumbent Prime Minister of Singapore drinking a glass of purified sewerage water.

The newspaper caption added that the refuse water had undergone a reliable purification process such that it was good for drinking and completely safe.

THE REPREHENSIBLE (*MAKRŪH*)

Makrūh according to the majority of leading schools refers to an act, object, or conduct that should be avoided but whose perpetrator is not liable to punishment and does not incur moral blame either. The *Ḥanafīs* are in agreement with the majority position in respect of only one of the two varieties of *makrūh*, namely that of *makrūh* for the sake of purity (*makrūh tanzīhī*), but not with regard to what they classify as *makrūh taḥrīmī* (*makrūh* closer to *ḥarām*), which does entail moral blame but not punishment. The leading schools are in agreement that one who avoids *makrūh* merits praise and gains closeness to God.[52] *Makrūh* is often described as the lowest degree of prohibition and, in this sense, it is used as a convenient category the jurists have employed for matters that fall between the *ḥalāl* and *ḥarām*, matters that are definitely discouraged but where the evidence to establish them as *ḥarām* is less than certain. Matters of this kind are conveniently placed under *makrūh* for lack mainly of a better alternative. The *ḥanafī* category of *makrūh tanzīhī* is subsumed under *mubāḥ* by the majority.

According to the Ḥanafīs, an act is *ḥarām* when it is decreed in definitive terms, but when there is an element of weakness in the prohibitive language of the Qur'an or hadith, the matter falls under *makrūh taḥrīmī*, that is *makrūh* close to *ḥarām*. For example, it is *makrūh taḥrīmī* to make an offer of betrothal to a woman who is already betrothed to another man. The reason for this is that the hadith proscribing this is a solitary (*āḥād*) hadith, which is not altogether devoid of doubt in respect of authenticity.[53] There is much disagreement among jurists about *makrūh* in foodstuffs and other substances for human consumption, but most would include rotten meat that develops an offensive smell, water of a well in the midst of a graveyard, and unsupervised cattle and poultry that feed on impurities and filth such that changes of taste and smell in them may be detectable. The relevant hadiths also include the milk of such animals.[54] This impurity is, however, removed when animals are kept away from their dirty habitats for a number of days (three for poultry, four for sheep and goats, and ten for camels and cows). The preferred position of the majority of schools on this issue, however, departs from these specifications and merely advises isolation until the offensive signs and smells are no longer present.[55] It is *makrūh* to consume the meat of donkeys and drink their milk; drinking the urine of camel and consumption of horse meat is likewise disapproved – especially in wartime when horses may be needed.

Certain types of food are held to be reprehensible if taken under certain circumstances but which are basically good for consumption. The Prophet thus said: "Whenever you consume raw onion or garlic, you should not go to the mosque for congregation prayers."[56] These items should not be consumed when their odour becomes offensive to others in the mosque setting as is stated in the hadith but also elsewhere when close contact with others is likely to have a similar effect.

While it is reprehensible to use the tusk of elephant as a tool for slaughter, there are conflicting views on the matter. It is also reprehensible to slaughter an animal without the intention of having it as food for consumption, for it would mean killing an animal without a valid purpose. Furthermore, hunting of young birds for pleasure is reprehensible. All living beings have their own position in the order of creation and humans are responsible for the protection of animals at their disposal and control, including animals' health and adequate feeding. It is a part of our responsibility as God's vicegerents in the earth to care for the environment and well-being of all the earth's inhabitants.

According to al-Shāṭibī (d.1388/790), the sin for the performance of *makrūh* and *ḥarām* is not equivalent to the sin for acts and conduct that serve as the means toward them, and which are not the ends or objectives in themselves. The degree of prohibition and repulsiveness of acts that serve as means toward a sinful act will accordingly be less than committing the acts which are the ends in themselves. *Makrūh* may as such serve and qualify as a means to *ḥarām*.[57]

Certain organs of lawfully slaughtered and *ḥalāl* animals have also been declared non *ḥalāl*. These include blood, the phallus, testicles, vagina, glands, gall bladder and bile, which are considered by the Ḥanafīs to be *makrūh taḥrīmī* due to the fact that the prohibitory hadith text on them is a solitary hadith that is not entirely free of all doubt.[58] The textual authority for *makrūh* may consist of a reference to something that is specifically identified as *makrūh*, or may be so identified by a word or words that convey an equivalent meaning. The work *makrūh* occurs in its literal sense in the following verse: "All of these are evil and abomination in the sight of your Lord" (*al-Isrā'*, 17:38). The reference here is to a number of things, including walking on the earth with insolence, taking a stand on a matter without adequate knowledge, failure to give due measurement and weight, and failure to keep one's promise. In another Qur'anic passage, it is enjoined: "And seek not the bad to give in charity when you would not take it for yourselves save with disdain" (*al-Baqarah*, 2:267). The subject also falls under the Qur'an text that "he (the Prophet) forbids to them (Muslims) all that which is unclean (*khabā'ith*)"(*Al-Aʿrāf*, 7:157). But this verse is also a manifest text (*ẓāhir*) which is in the nature of probability. It is not certain, in other words, that the six items were actually meant to be included under the *khabā'ith*. The prohibitive view also holds these organs to be abhorrent to people of sound nature (*al-ṭabā'iʿ al-salīmah*).[59] The other three schools are less restrictive, but their preferred position also considers the organs in question to be *makrūh*.[60] As for the use of rennet (*minfaḥah*) from the stomach of cattle for use in fermentation and processing cheese, if it is taken from a lawfully slaughtered animal, it is *ḥalāl* by consensus; but if taken from carrion, it is non *ḥalāl* according to the majority, but *ḥalāl* according to the Ḥanafīs on the ground of an analogy they draw between this and the milk of such animals.[61] Other instances of *makrūh* to be noted in conjunction with the rituals of slaughter include rough handling (such as dragging the animal by its feet), abandoning the *tasmiyah* (i.e. reciting the name God) according to the Shāfiʿīs and Mālikīs, slaughter in front of another animal, the use of bones and stones as cutting tools, cutting or skinning the animal before the complete exit of life, not facing the *qiblah*, and citing the name of Muhammad next to that of Allah. The Mālikīs do not stipulate facing the *qiblah* as a requirement of slaughter due to the absence of textual evidence on this. The basis of this they say is a weak analogy that is drawn between the obligatory prayer (salah) and slaughter, which are altogether two different things.[62]

The question of tobacco and smoking is more complex. Smoking is undoubtedly widespread among Muslims, yet, scholars have different opinions over it. The majority hold smoking to be reprehensible. It is a waste of money and it has no nutritional value, nor does it have any medically proven benefit. Its health risks are almost certain in connection with such diseases as lung cancer, heart attack, and emphysema among the smokers. To abstain from smoking is therefore highly recommended; smoking should in some circumstances be even banned altogether.[63] The risk of declaring smoking *ḥarām* is the fear that by doing so, one is declaring millions of smoking Muslims as sinners and transgressors, which is hardly advisable. More importantly perhaps is the absence of a textual injunction on the issue, and the juridical principle that arm can only be created based on the authority of a clear text.

The textual authority for *makrūh* may consist of a reference in the sources of Shariʿah to something which is specifically identified as *makrūh*, or may have been so identified by words that convey an equivalent meaning. There is a hadith, for example, in which the Prophet discouraged any prayers at midday until the decline of the sun, with the exception of Friday prayers. The actual words used in the hadith are that the Prophet disliked (*kariha al-nabiy*) prayers at that particular time.[64] An equivalent term to *makrūh* occurs, for example, in the hadith which says: "The most abominable of permissible things (*abghaḍ al-ḥalāl*) in the sight of God is divorce."[65] *Makrūh* may also be conveyed in the form of a prohibition but in a language that indicates only reprehensibility. An example of this is the Qur'anic text which provided, in an address to the believers warning them against excessive questioning "O ye who believe! Ask not questions about which, if made plain to you, you may dislike it" (*al-Mā'idah*, 5:101). Another illustration of this is the saying of the Prophet: "Leave that which you are doubtful about in favour of that which you do not doubt."[66]

THE RECOMMENDED (*MANDŪB*)

Mandūb (also known as *sunnah, mustaḥab, nafl*) denotes an act or conduct that the Shariʿah has recommended, but which is not binding. To comply with the *mandūb* earns one spiritual reward but no punishment is imposed for its neglect. *Mandūb* is the opposite of *makrūh*, and this means that avoidance of *makrūh* amounts to *mandūb*. Handling the slaughtered animal with clemency and care is *mandūb*, and rough handling is *makrūh*. To set up a charitable endowment (*waqf*), attend to the sick, and honour one's neighbour and one's guest are all recommended. If the *mandūb* is an act which the Prophet has performed on some occasions but omitted on others, it is called sunnah, which is also of two types: It is emphatic sunnah (*sunnah mu'akkadah*, also known as *sunnah al-hudā*) if the Prophet has performed it regularly, or which he has strongly recommended, such as attending the mosque congregation for obligatory prayers (salah), and calling out the call for prayer (*adhān*) preceding it. To perform an act of merit, such as offering two units of sunnah prior to the obligatory early and late afternoon (ẓuhr or ʿaṣr) prayers, or being generous in charity above the level of the obligatory alms tax (zakah) are examples of supererogatory sunnah, or *sunnah ghayr mu'akkadah*. The schools of law have employed a variety of other expressions for *mandūb*, such as *taṭawwuʿ*, *faḍīlah*, *iḥsān* and *raghā'ib* with finer distinctions that often consist of sound advice and cultural refinement.[67]

The recommendable and reprehensible (*mandūb, makrūh*) respectively are conceptual antonyms in that the one is, for the most part, the opposite of the other. Doing the opposite of *makrūh* thus amounts to *mandūb* and vice versa. The recommendable in dietary substances in Islam relates to some food items that are either mentioned in the Qur'an in a positive context or which were favoured by the Prophet, such as honey, figs, olives, dates and milk. The first three are mentioned in the Qur'an whereas dates and milk were liked by the Prophet, and it is recommended also to open one's fast, during Ramadan for instance, with dates.[68]

Much of the fiqh information on recommendable in foodstuffs and drinks also relate to mannerism, supplication and thanksgiving and the use or otherwise of certain utensils. Thus it is known that the Prophet usually started his meal with the supplication "All praise and thanks to Allah who has satisfied our needs and quenched our thirst. His favours cannot be compensated for nor denied."[69] He recommended the same after eating, and advised those who forgot to say it at the outset to say it anytime during the meal. Whatever the Prophet has practiced or recommended would thus be *mandūb*. Reports indicate that the Prophet used to wash his hands before and after taking a meal, and that he took his meal while sitting and started taking food with his right hand. He has also left us with the instruction to take food which is nearest to where we are seated first, and one who eats with the hand should also take food from the near side of the dish and not the middle. He has further advised against blowing on the food as this could taint the food with traces of saliva and unpleasant breath. He used to drink while sitting, which is the recommended position, although he has on certain occasions been seen to have drank water while standing. He has similarly advised against drinking directly from the pitcher, which would be reprehensible, for evidently hygienic reasons. The hadith reports further indicate that the Prophet strongly discouraged the use of gold and silver utensils, in his quest, presumably, of modesty and avoidance of vainglory and extravagance. Gold and silver were declared as units of value and were consequently used as currency in those days.[70]

THE 'GREY AREAS': DOUBTFUL MATTERS (*AL-SHUBUHĀT, MASHBŪH, MASHKŪK*)

These are the intervening (and often undetermined) matters that fall between the *ḥalāl* and *ḥarām*. Doubts may arise due mainly to two factors: Either the source evidence of the Shariʿah is not free from doubt in respect of meaning or authenticity, or else its application to a particular subject or case is uncertain.

The Qur'an (*Āl ʿImrān*, 3:7) itself has confirmed that some parts of it are inherently doubtful and refers to them as *mutashābihāt*. The precise meaning of certain expressions, words or phrases, of the Qur'an under the category of *mutashābihāt* is not known to anyone but God the Most High. For instance, a number of surahs, nineteen to be precise, of the Qur'an begin with abbreviated letters, known as *muqaṭṭaʿāt*, which are a mystery and thus inherently ambiguous – although some commentators say that the Prophet knew their meaning. The Prophet has acknowledged this in a long hadith to the effect that *ḥalāl* and *ḥarām* had been made clear from one another but that "in between them there are the doubtful matters which are not known to most people whether they are *ḥalāl* or *ḥarām*. One who avoids them for the purity of one's religion and honour would have saved oneself [...]."[71] To avoid doubt, and to make an effort to stay clear of it, is thus conducive to piety and one's good name and reputation. This much is indicated in the wording of the hadith, which speaks of requital and absolvement (*istibrā'*), and the course of action recommend concerning it is to take caution over doubtful matters.

The advice so conveyed in this hadith is, in al-Qaradawi's view, one of "obstructing the means to an evil end (*sadd al-dharā'iʿ*), which is informed by a certain insight into the health of one's personality and character ...."[72] Indulgence in *mashbūhāt* can, in other words, lead to *ḥarām* and the advice is to block the means that leads to *ḥarām*. In yet another hadith, Muslims are instructed to "abandon that which is doubtful to you in favour of that which is clear of doubt."[73] The possibilities of indulgence in doubt have undoubtedly increased in our times. Today, doubts arise, for instance, about factory farming where animal remains are fed to other animals, and the use of hormones and antibiotics also present difficulties in verifying whether the meat one buys or consumes is *mashbūh* or *ḥalāl*. Factory practices may also fail the test of compatibility with the Islamic principle of compassion. Definitive answers to these questions need to be informed by expert opinion and scientific evidence. The frequent incidence of BSE ('mad-cow disease') in some countries[74] has also raised questions about feeding and rearing methods and the wholesomeness of meat of such animals. These are genuine doubts that merit investigation and research.

According to a legal maxim of fiqh, "when the *ḥalāl* and *ḥarām* are mixed up, the *ḥarām* prevails."[75] In other words, when available evidence can imply both permissibility and prohibition, the latter prevails. While quoting this in his *Al-Ashbāh wa al-Naẓā'ir*, al-Suyūṭī mentions that his maxim is based on a hadith to the same effect. The hadith thus provided "When there is a mixing of *ḥalāl* and *ḥarām*, the latter prevails." However, Muslim scholars including Abū al-Faḍl al-ʿIrāqī, Tāj al-Dīn al-Subkī (d.1369/771) and Abū Bakr al-Bayhaqī (d.1064/456) considered this to be a weak hadith due to disruption in its chain of transmission.[76] Yet in circumstances where the amount of mixing and scope of confusion is slight to negligible, the legal maxim under review may also be of doubtful application. Some scholars have gone on record, moreover, to exonerate situations that involve minimal and sometimes unavoidable amounts of mixture with forbidden stuffs.

Confusion may also arise due to the existence of two divergent hadith reports, or two conflicting analogies: one prohibitive, and the other permissive, the former prevails over the latter. Prohibition in this case takes priority over permissibility. This is the purport also of the legal maxim that "prevention of harm takes priority over realisation of benefit."[77] The doubt that arises over a text may be genuine (*ḥaqīqī*), such as ambiguity in the actual wording of a hadith, or it may be relative and metaphorical (*iḍāfī*, *majāzī*), and doubt arises in their application to a particular case. In all of these, an opportunity may arise for fresh interpretation and ijtihad, which should be attempted and an effort should be made to secure that which is in the public interest and *maṣlaḥah*. Thus in cases of confusion between lawfully slaughtered meat and carrion, the prohibitive position prevails and consumption is consequently not recommended. Similarly in the case of confusion arising between revenues from *ribā* and from a lawful sale, one should exercise caution on the side of avoidance. In the case of the hybrid breeding of animals, such as between a horse and a mule, the issue is considered to be non-*ḥalāl*. Most jurists would, however, take the mother's side as the stronger indicator of permissibility: If the mother is *ḥalāl*, the issue is also considered *ḥalāl*.

Should there be a mixture of two varieties of food, one *ḥalāl* and the other *ḥarām*, two situations may initially arise: Either the separation of the two parts is not feasible, such as when wine, blood or urine is mixed with water – then the *ḥarām* prevails over *ḥalāl*; or else the two parts can be separated, as when an insect or unclean substance falls on solidified butter – the object itself and its surrounding parts are removed and the rest becomes *ḥalāl*. However, if the mixture is of very small quantities that are hardly detectable and establishment of complete purity is not devoid of hardship, such as the remains of small amounts of alcohol in cooking utensils in big hotels, the doubt in them may be overlooked but avoidance is preferable.[78]

FOOD ENHANCERS AND ADDITIVES

As a general rule, the principles that guide the processing of foodstuffs, such as meats and beverages, are also applicable to food ingredients, enhancers and additives. Muslims are consequently under obligation to abide by the rulings of Shariʿah concerning foodstuffs, additives, cosmetics and medicine, which may not be conducive to their health and well being. However in some circumstances, often specified by the Shariʿah, the legal maxim that "necessities make the unlawful lawful" may apply. Similarly all things are juridically clean, as explained above, except for those that are declared otherwise. To ascertain the rulings of Shariʿah on a certain ingredient or additive, the sources of these substances must naturally be taken into consideration.

Any food ingredient and additive derived from a *ḥalāl* source are also *ḥalāl* provided they are good and wholesome. It is safe to say that food ingredients and additives derived from plants and chemicals that are clear of doubt, *ḥalāl* synthetic food, eggs, fish and duly slaughtered meat derivatives are *ḥalāl*. All derivatives of fish and vegetables are *ḥalāl*; and all that may be derived from cows, sheep, goats and other *ḥalāl* animals are lawful for consumption provided they are not dead, nor added to, nor mixed with, that which is *ḥarām* by itself.

Some ingredients and additives are added to food to preserve it from spoilage, to improve its color and flavor for consumption and texture, and indeed, to extend its freshness. Some of these additives are natural, such as sugar, salt, honey etc., while others are synthetic, such as sodium bicarbonate, sodium nitrate and synthetic vitamins. However, in the light of the rules and regulations that protect human health and the lives of the consumers, a good number of incidents have been specified and recorded. Some of the chemicals used in food processing have thus proven to be injurious and harmful to health and are therefore decidedly questionable. A number of these additives are carcinogenic, and contain toxic substances that may affect human sexual behavior and health.[79] If those ingredients and additives prove, through reliable testing, not to be injurious, but are helpful for human health and well-being, they may be consumed. However, if they prove harmful to health, they may be considered as either *makrūh* or *makrūh taḥrīmī*, and even *ḥarām* in the event where there is definitive proof.

MASHBŪH INGREDIENTS AND ADDITIVES

While many additives and ingredients can be clearly identified to be *ḥalāl* or *ḥarām*, there are others which are not so clear. Substances of this kind are questionable and doubtful, and more information may be needed to categorise them as either *ḥalāl*, *ḥarām* or *makrūh*. Food falling under this category should preferably be avoided on grounds of purity and integrity of one's faith. It is advisable perhaps to place the doubtful substance under the category of *makrūh* until further information becomes available to clarify the position. This includes ingredients such as gelatin, emulsifiers, fat and enzymes of doubtful origins. All of these are doubtful. Many of them do in fact have alternatives that are either *ḥalāl* or vegetarian products that can just as easily be used in their place.[80]

Imported meats may also be put under doubtful foodstuffs. Questions as to the origin of the imported foodstuffs and food produced or processed in doubtful conditions may be discussed under four basic categories as follows:

a) Muslim jurists are in agreement to the effect that meats and other foodstuffs imported from non-Muslim countries, such as Europe and America, where the majority are either Jews or Christians are lawful provided they are not derived from *ḥarām* sources and animals. It is not recommended to investigate whether the meats were slaughtered according to Islamic rituals or not. This is because permissibility is the basic principle that applies to slaughter and foodstuffs of the people of scripture, as confirmed by a clear text of the Qur'an (*al-Mā'idah*, 5:5), except where there is a proof to the contrary. Muslims are not, however, permitted to eat meat over which an invocation is made to any deity other than Allah.[81] Therefore, unfounded doubts that advise abstinence are of no account and permissibility prevails. If it is known that pronouncing the name of God on an animal is deliberately avoided, the flesh of that animal is not *ḥalāl* according the majority of jurists.[82]

b) Meat and meat products imported from the Zoroastrian (*majūsī*) origins and others who do not believe in the concept of ritual slaughter is also forbidden for Muslims according to the majority of the Muslim jurists, who hold that most of these People are Polytheists and disbelievers. Another opinion holds that they are also counted among the people of scripture; hence, their slaughter becomes *ḥalāl* by analogy. It is reported that Ibn Ḥazm al-Ẓāhirī (d.1064/456) considered the Zoroastrians to be included among the People of Scripture and consequently applied the same rules that apply to the latter also to Zoroastrians.[83]

c) The doubtful varieties of meat products can include mistakenly labelled meat products as *ḥalāl* when these are in fact not *ḥalāl*. It makes no difference whether labelling is intentional or otherwise. It is also possible that purely sale and marketing factors drive these decisions in total disregard of Shariʿah rules. When a meat product is labelled as *ḥalāl* with no reference to the certifying authority, the chances are high that the meat in question is mislabelled and therefore falls under the *mashbūhāt* as already discussed. Research findings indicate that a producer looking for *ḥalāl* meat as an ingredient must not assume that a meat item labelled as *ḥalāl* is authentically *ḥalāl*. To be certain, a *ḥalāl* certificate should be requested for every lot of meat to be used. Since meat is the most critical ingredient the supervising authority should evaluate the supplier or recommend another supplier. Market survey has also noted Muslim customer responses that they will not buy minced meat from non-*ḥalāl* stores. This is because several large and small food chains are known to mix pork with beef. Even in Malaysia, according to a report a factory producing dried tofu, apparently with *ḥalāl* certification, was operating next to a pig farm in the Cheras district of Kuala Lumpur. The product was found to be made in doubtful conditions, with only a thin wall separating the pig farm and the factory. Several stray dogs were also seen roaming the place, and a wood-processing factory in the area produced massive amounts of dust in a tight space. "It is believed the *ḥalāl* logo by JAKIM (Islamic Development Department Malaysia) that is used by the company for its product packaging is fake".[84] It took some time for JAKIM to take action. Its Director General Othman Mustapha announced that starting 1 January 2013, the use of '*ḥalāl*' logos, symbols and words such as 'Muslim food' and 'Ramadan buffet' that confuse Muslim consumers will be banned. Any organisation found guilty may face up to RM200,000 (about $65,000) for the first offense or up to RM500,000 for the second and subsequent offenses. It was further announced that all imported food items to be declared *ḥalāl* should also have the *ḥalāl* logo and certification issued by the authorities in the producing countries recognized by JAKIM.[85]

d) Some doubt in the *ḥalāl* identification process also emanates from the fact that non-Muslims tend to dominate the industry in so many ways. With the exception of the act of slaughtering that must be done by a Muslim person, according to regulations, the other segments of industry remain open for non-Muslims. The supply chain like farming, food manufacturing, commodity trading, logistics, restaurants, hotels and retail chains are dominated by non-Muslim countries and businesses. Muslim countries and companies have, in fact, only a limited role in the *ḥalāl* food value chain.[86]

INGREDIENTS AND ADDITIVES THAT MAY BE CONSIDERED UNLAWFUL

It is to be stated at the outset that recourse to legal stratagems (*ḥiyal*) that seek to procure *ḥarām* under a different guise or name is also forbidden. This includes ingredients that originate in *ḥarām*, such as pork, pork by-products, and meats which are not ritually purified. Using substances derived from forbidden animals, or derivatives that have undergone chemical transformation, such as gelatin used in the production of drug capsules, derived from organs or tissues of pigs; the majority of *ʿulamāʾ* hold that they are forbidden. Foodstuffs containing pig fat which does not undergo denaturation, such as some varieties of cheese, vegetable oil, butter, cream, biscuit, chocolate and ice-cream, are also prohibited. All of this must be avoided, barring a situation that may warrant an exception due to "necessity." Necessity is admittedly not always predictable. But as there is no pressing case of public interest or necessity to warrant their consumption since the lives of people do not depend on them, and avoiding them does not lead to disruption and chaos of normal order, this opinion stands. Avoiding those items has no adverse effect on the integrity of religion, life, intellect, lineage and property either. Thus to avoid them becomes the obvious conclusion.

As an ingredient or additive in medicine, alcohol is generally forbidden due to its intoxicating nature. Exceptions to this rule are such situations in which alcohol-free medicine is not available, and for medicines currently in production that contain a very small measure of alcohol for the purpose of non-sedating preservative or solvent, until an alternative is made available. All narcotic drugs and substances are prohibited and under no circumstances are they permissible except for specific medical treatment that may be determined by qualified physicians. The Shariʿah grounds of some of the foregoing are expounded in our discussion of *ḥarām* in the following pages.

Foods containing even a small amount of wine are to be avoided, including chocolates and drinks or foods tinged with alcohol. Intoxicants are thus forbidden in either large amounts or small,[87] as per an explicit ruling of the Shariʿah. The rule of exceptional permissibility is not applicable here due to the absence of the necessary factor.

There are many medical issues that are connected to the rules of necessity. For instance, some medicines and mouthwashes contain alcohol; thus if one can find a non-alcoholic alternative, then that is preferable. It should be noted, however, that only ethyl alcohol (such as methylated spirits and ethanol – the alcohol found in alcoholic drinks) are intoxicating and are therefore *ḥarām*.[88] There is no problem in using perfumes or scents (e.g. Eau de Cologne) in which alcohol is used as a solvent for manufacturing of fragrances or aromatic substances, or in using body lotions which contain alcohol.

In contrast, small quantities of alcohol can be found in certain *ḥalāl* foods, such as bread and soy sauce. They may sometimes contain minute amounts of alcohol as a result of a natural reaction between certain chemicals during the manufacturing process (as opposed to alcohol drinks being deliberately added to food to add flavour), and so could not be classified as *ḥarām*.

REQUIREMENTS OF A VALID SLAUGHTER

The rituals of a valid slaughter and its accompanying requirements of cleanliness are fairly well-known to the *ḥalāl* industry, and the prevailing practices of various Muslim countries, although different in respect of details, are also deemed to be compliant with the Shariʿah guidelines. The foregoing discussion indicated some of the features of a valid slaughter and what may be regarded to be *mandūb* or *makrūh* therein. The discussion that follows highlights the Shariʿah requirements of a valid slaughter, and also touches on some disputed issues:

1. The element of intention: A lawful slaughter occurs only when it is with the intention of a valid use, and not merely to kill an animal for the sake of killing. Hence, a slaughter without such an intention is non *ḥalāl*.
2. Reciting the name of Allah or *tasmiyah* at the time of slaughter is obligatory (*wājib*) according to the majority of *madhāhib*, whereas the Shāfiʿīs consider it to be recommended (*mandūb*) and abandoning it as *makrūh*. All schools would, on the other hand, exonerate from these requirements the case of genuine forgetfulness without intentional preclusion. It is noteworthy that the Qur'an stipulated *tasmiyah* for slaughter in contrast to the pre-Islamic Arabian practice of reciting the names of ancient deities. It is also instructive to note that mankind is not naturally entitled to take the life of an animal unless it is with the permission of the Creator, and *tasmiyah* is an affirmation and acknowledgement of that. Richard Foltz draws the following conclusions from his review of the evidence: "First, the tradition takes the relationship between humans and other animal species quite seriously. Second, animals are seen as having feelings and interests of their own. And third, the overriding ethos enjoined upon humans is one of compassionate consideration."[89]
3. Ritual slaughter is allowed by a person who is a Muslim or follower of a revealed scripture, including Christians and Jews. The Qur'an has thus affirmed that "the food of the *ahl al-kitāb*" – such as Christians and Jews – is *ḥalāl* for Muslims, and vice versa (*al-Mā'idah*, 5:5).[90] The food and slaughter of the *ahl al-kitāb* is *ḥalāl* to us generally even if they omit the *tasmiyah*, or even if they recite the name of Jesus Christ or Moses. Some Muslim jurists have disputed this last position, but since the Qur'anic permission is conveyed in unqualified terms, it is *ḥalāl* for Muslims to consume their food and accept their slaughter.[91]
4. According to a general consensus of the leading schools of Islamic law, severance is required of the four vital passages in the slaughter of animals, namely the trachea, oesophagus and jugular veins. Some minor disagreements have arisen to the effect that slaughter occurs even if the oesophagus is not cut, though it is recommended to sever the four sections all at once.

The following slaughter practices are recommended (*mandūb*):

- Recitation of both *tasmiyah* and the phrase 'God is Greatest' i.e. *Allāhu Akbar* known for short as *takbīr*.
- Completion of slaughter in daylight so as to prevent error in the correct procedures.
- Facing the *qiblah* toward Mecca, although the Mālikī school does not require this.
- Except for the camel (which requires *naḥr*, as opposed to *dhabḥ*, in standing position with a left leg tied up), all animals should rest on the left side with their heads lifted upwards.
- Clemency to the animal and avoidance of rough handling.[92]

The following are considered reprehensible (*makrūh*) in the slaughter rituals:

- Slaughter by a disabled person.
- Abandoning the *tasmiyah* according to those who do not consider it obligatory, namely the Shāfiʿīs and some Mālikīs.
- Facing the animal in a direction other than the *qiblah*.
- *Naḥr* of the cattle and *dhabḥ* of the camel; the normal method is in the reverse order.
- Inflicting pain on the animal such as by severing the head completely or breaking the skull, dragging the animal, and slaughter from the back of the neck.
- Slaughter by a dull and unsuitable knife.[93]

Certain aspects of the distinction between the *makrūh* and *ḥarām* are not always accurately stated. Note for instance that some individual writers have haphazardly labelled as *ḥarām* that which may actually amount to no more than *makrūh*. This often happens with some so-called religious leaders who pronounce *ḥarām* all too readily for greater emphasis. This is to be strictly avoided as per clear textual warning of the Qur'an as follows: "And let not your tongues describe in falsehood that 'This is lawful and this is forbidden,' for this is tantamount to ascribing lies to Allah" (*al-Naḥl*, 16:116). In his book, *Al-Ḥalāl wa al-Ḥarām fī al-Islam* (p. 27) al-Qaradawi discusses this in some details to say that the leading Imams of jurisprudence were extremely reluctant to declare anything as *ḥarām*. When they had occasion to proscribe something in a fatwa they chose to declare it as *makrūh*. "This is not an issue but declaring something *ḥarām* is a serious one."

Some of the *ḥalāl* procedural guidelines also stipulate ritual cleansing of animals hides that have not undergone *ḥalāl* slaughtering. This is evidently not a requirement of the renowned hadith, recorded by Muslim and Abū Dāwūd, which provides: "when any hide is tanned, it is purified."[94] The ruling of this hadith is general (*ʿāmm*) and unqualified, hence it includes "all hides even of the dog and the pig. This is the position of the Ẓāhirī school, also recorded by Abū Yūsuf, the disciple of Abū Ḥanīfah, and it is preferred by al-Shawkānī."[95] Furthermore, it is quite obvious from our perusal of the relevant rules that the Shariʿah prohibition of carrion is confined to eating and does not extend to the use of its hide, horns, bones and hair, all of which are permitted. They are valuable assets or *māl* as they carry a market value, and if they could be put to a good use, they should not be wasted.[96]

THE ROLE OF CUSTOM (*ʿURF*) IN THE DETERMINATION OF VALUES

General custom (*ʿurf, ʿādah*) is a recognized source of law and judgment in Islamic jurisprudence. It is defined as "recurrent practices that are acceptable to people of sound nature."[97] To constitute a valid basis of judgment, custom must be sound and reasonable and must not contravene a clear text or principle of the Shariʿah. Custom is rejected if it is in conflict with a clear injunction of the Shariʿah, such as some tribal practices that deny women their rights of inheritance, or local communities that consume the flesh of snakes and monkeys. In the event, however, of a partial conflict between a text and custom, the latter may qualify or specify the former. A valid ruling of custom often takes precedence over the normal rules, or the ruling of analogy (*qiyās*). This is because custom represents the people's convenience, and adopting it is often tantamount to removal of hardship, which is one of the expressed purposes of the Shariʿah. It is commonly acknowledged that a great deal of the fiqh rules and the rulings of ijtihad have taken their cues from the prevailing practices of their time.

The role of custom is evidently recognized in the evaluation of the *mandūb* and *makrūh* in foodstuffs, which often correspond with what is approved or disapproved by the people of sound nature (often referred to as the *ahl al-ʿurf*). The law may recognize some food as *ḥalāl* but may not be liked by the people and may thus, to all intents and purposes, be relegated to the category of *makrūh*, or else that a *mubāḥ* is elevated to the level of *mandūb* by the people's preference for it. For instance, seafood is all declared to be clean and edible by the clear text of a hadith, and there is little doubt that this would include such items as prawn and shark. But prawn is not taken, for instance, by the Ḥanafī Muslims of Pakistan and many people have similar reservations about sharks. There is in principle no Shariʿah objection to customary practices of this kind. When people of sound nature approve of such practices, then according to a leading maxim of fiqh: "Custom is the basis of judgment (*al-ʿādatu muḥakkamatun*)."[98] Custom also determines the question, for instance, of whether or not an object is regarded as valuable property, or *māl*, that carries market value. For instance, honey bees and silk worms were at one time not regarded to be valuable assets, or *māl* but were later determined to qualify as *māl* by the people's usage and acceptance of them as such, and a fatwa was accordingly issued in its support. It is to be noted, however, that custom is changeable with the advancement of science and technology, which often set in place new practices that may soon gain wide recognition and acceptance. People's tastes regarding foodstuffs are also affected by the media and advertisements and so forth. New practices take hold among people as and when they prove to be convenient, which is often reflected in their lifestyle and food varieties. All of this is likely to carry the seal of Shariʿah approval if no principles have been contravened. Furthermore, people's approval and disapproval also play a role in the determination of what may be regarded as a compelling necessity (*ḍarūrah*).

MEAT, SEAFOOD, AND DAIRY PRODUCTS

Having discussed the Shariᶜah scale of five values and its applications to the subject of our concern, what follows in the next few pages is a continuation of the same discussion albeit with regard to specific animal varieties. Generally goats, beef, lamb, rabbit, buffalo, deer, cattle, and camels are *ḥalāl* animals for slaughter and consumption. Permitted birds include chicken, fowl, quails, turkey, hens, geese and ducks.

Ḥarām meat and meat products include pork and all pork-derived products and ingredients. Swine is held unlawful for consumption by all Muslims without exception. It is also *ḥarām* to raise, transport or trade in porcine products and derivatives that are meant for consumption.

Also excluded from the *ḥalāl* category are beasts of prey having talons and fangs, such as lions, hyenas, wolves, dogs, tigers, foxes and jackals as well as domesticated donkeys. Non-*ḥalāl* birds include those which prey on the flesh of dead carcasses, such as vultures, crows, eagles, falcons, pelicans and other scavengers. The milk and eggs of prohibited animals and birds are also forbidden for consumption. With minor exceptions of hunting, animals which are not properly slaughtered are also non-*ḥalāl*. This includes improperly slaughtered animals as well as ones that die naturally from disease, altercations with other animals or cruelty by human actors.

Fish and seafood including shellfish are *ḥalāl*. However, no dying fish must be made to suffer. Thus it is unlawful to bludgeon a live fish or marine creatures, nor must they be cut open while alive. It shall not be cooked alive, but should be left to die by itself.

Milk and dairy products such as cheese and yogurt must not contain gelatin unless that gelatin is known to be from *ḥalāl* sources. Many cheeses contain rennet and other enzymes that are derived from animals. It is important to assure that these are derived from *ḥalāl* animals or from microbial or plant sources.

Fresh fruits and vegetables are all *ḥalāl*. Processed fruits and vegetables may be unacceptable if they are produced in processing plants using non-*ḥalāl* oil, fats, preservatives, flavoring, coloring etc.

The procedures used in producing these items do not, however, involve on-site Muslim supervision. Yet it is prudent that the producer obtains *ḥalāl* certification for its products and procedures.

Bakery goods carry particular *ḥalāl* concerns. The production process of bakery goods must not use hidden ingredients, fillers, alcohol-based or animal-based ingredients that may render the product questionable and doubtful. It is important to assure that the additive, colorants and preservatives are from *ḥalāl* sources and are processed according to approved procedures without the usage of alcohol-based ingredients.

THE *ḤALĀL* INDUSTRY IN MALAYSIA

Malaysia holds a special position in the global *ḥalāl* market. Shafie and Othman reported from their consumer behavior survey that for the Muslim consumers of Malaysia, *ḥalāl* is a key requirement. *Ḥalāl* brands and certification originate in different places, yet some of the local brands appear to have developed their own niche. In general, Muslim consumers in Malaysia look for the authentic *ḥalāl* certification by Malaysia's Department of Islamic Development (JAKIM) of the Prime Minister's Office. In 2004 when Malaysia launched its first Malaysia International *ḥalāl* Showcase (MIHAS) in Kuala Lumpur, the then Prime Minister Abdullah Ahmad Badawi in his speech declared that establishing Malaysia as a global *ḥalāl* hub was a major priority of the government and that MIHAS was the largest *ḥalāl* trade expo to be held anywhere in the world. *Ḥalāl* products and services in Malaysia cover a wide range of products that extend from food and beverage to accommodation, attire, insurance, financial products, cosmetics and personal hygiene.[99]

Malaysia's global *ḥalāl* hub concept aims to create opportunities for small and medium enterprises, or SMEs, to penetrate the *ḥalāl* markets in the Middle East, the OIC countries and elsewhere. The Federal Agricultural Marketing Authority (FAMA) estimated the market size for frozen food only to increase to MYR 193 billion by 2010. Yet actual developments have fallen short of meeting forecasts owing partly to the limited range of *ḥalāl* products in the market which are insufficient to cater for the demand. As of June 2011, the *ḥalāl* industry in Malaysia was estimated to be worth MYR 56 billion a year whereas for the global market it is estimated between US$ 2.5 trillion and US$ 2.7 trillion. In announcing these figures, the Deputy Minister of Trade and Industry, Mukhriz Mahathir, also revealed that Bumiputras (mainly native Malays) hold only 30 per cent of the 4,787 *ḥalāl* certificates so far issued by JAKIM to companies in the food and beverage industry. He noted that more non-Bumiputra companies were applying for *ḥalāl* certification. "This is despite the fact that being certified *ḥalāl* could be a ticket to growth outside Malaysia," Mukhriz Mahathir said adding "that the market potential for *ḥalāl* products is huge, especially in ASEAN, the Middle East and China... In China alone, there are good prospects for *ḥalāl* products, as four provinces there have a huge Muslim population with high purchasing power."[100] As part of its global *ḥalāl* hub policy, the Malaysian government has taken measures in both its Second Industrial Master Plan (1996-2005) and the National Agricultural Policy (1998-2010) to support the industry through the creation of a number of *ḥalāl* parks in the country. The state governments of Selangor, Kedah, Melaka, Negeri Sembilan, Perak, and Pahang have consequently established industrial *ḥalāl* parks in their respective states.[101] *Ḥalāl* parks are an effective instrument in clustering a big part of a *ḥalāl* value chain geographically in a country. Next to clustering advantages (like shortening of supply chain, cost reductions, innovations etc.), *ḥalāl* park can create a strong base for *ḥalāl* food products and allow enforcing of a common *ḥalāl* standard more efficiently. Malaysia has also formed a working group with several ASEAN countries to look into global issues such as the accreditation of *ḥalāl* food and registration list for *ḥalāl* preservatives.

JAKIM which supervises *ḥalāl* certification is entrusted with monitoring operations relating to *ḥalāl* production such as handling and packaging. Imported products are being certified by certain organisations accredited by JAKIM and government agencies such as the Department of Veterinary Services, and the Food Safety and Quality Division of the Ministry of Health, which issues clearance on suspected hazardous food substances. Malaysia's *ḥalāl* hub concept, moreover, aims to develop benchmarks for a Global *ḥalāl* Standard not only for food production and processing but also for pharmaceuticals, cosmetics and preservatives.[102] Once a *ḥalāl* certification is issued, the companies print and display the *ḥalāl* logo on their products and advertisements and at their company premises and outlets.

One of the reasons the Muslim and Bumiputra portion of the *ḥalāl* certificates is relatively small is the cost. It costs up to MYR 2,000 to get a two-year certificate for each product. To get a *ḥalāl* certificate is described as "a very meticulous process. Every single step of the business or manufacturing process will be evaluated and assessed, from the ingredients, process handling of the materials to the logistics."[103] Yet there are shortcomings in enforcement. Commentators have noted that lack of adequate enforcement by JAKIM personnel in monitoring the use of the *ḥalāl* logo has caused the public to question the authenticity of some of the products or services claimed to be *ḥalāl*.[104]

Ḥalāl foodstuffs according to Malaysia Standards are those substances that are permitted under the Shariʿah provided they fulfil the following conditions:

a) The food or its ingredients do not contain any component or product of animals that are non *ḥalāl* under Shariʿah law, or products of animals which are not slaughtered according to Shariʿah;
b) The food does not contain any ingredient that is considered as *najis* (filthy, impure) by Shariʿah;
c) That the food is safe and not harmful;
d) That the food or its ingredients do not contain any parts of the animal that are not permitted in Islam;
e) Foodstuffs that are not prepared, processed, or manufactured using equipment that already contaminated with *najis* according to the rulings of Shariʿah; and
f) Foodstuff that is not physically separated, during its preparation, processing, packing, storage, or transportation, from any other

food which does not meet the requirements stated in (a), (b), (c), (d) or (e) or anything that is considered as *najis* by the Shariʿah.

Based on these standards, it can be concluded that *ḥalāl* foodstuffs and certified substances and products in Malaysia do not consist of, nor contain anything that is *ḥarām* or *najis* according to Shariʿah law. When these standards are carefully observed, the certification issued by the authorised agency establishes the Shariʿah permissibility and *ḥalāl* status of the substances concerned.

By their express acknowledgement, these standards are developed to safeguard the life and well-being of the consumers and the public at large, and also to promote and facilitate domestic and international trade. It is a means also of promoting and consolidating international cooperation in food safety and health for the benefit of all.

ISLAM AND SCIENCE

Islam and science are too broad and also too important to be treated in a short passage intended merely to identify what bearings they may have on the *ḥalāl* and *ḥarām* in Islam. However, the first question that arises concerns the basic premise of these concepts: *ḥalāl* and *ḥarām* are evidently not determined by reference only to human reason or scientific knowledge, but a combination of these and the guidance mainly of divine revelation (*waḥy*). Worship matters (*ʿibādāt*) are normally determined by the Shariʿah independently of scientific evidence, and this could also be said of a limited number of dietary restrictions Islam has imposed – even though there may be some scientific justification for them. Having said this, Islam is on the whole receptive to scientific evidence. If one considers the Islamic prohibition of carrion, spilt blood, alcohol and pig meat for consumption, most of these, if not all, can perhaps stand the test of scientific knowledge. Scientific rationality essentially confines reality to the data of sense perception, which precludes metaphysical reality and revealed knowledge as well as some of the nonphysical sides of the human existence (such as reducing intelligence to the level of neural chemistry where mental and behavioral phenomena are understood merely as manifestations of physical processes).

Islamic juristic thought recognizes various levels of distinctions with a view to addressing temporal reality within its own parameters. For instance, the distinction between Shariʿah and fiqh did not exist during the first century of the advent of Islam, and the triple division of the Shariʿah into theology (*kalām*), morality (*akhlāq*) and fiqh (practical rulings) also developed at a later stage. A certain level of separation was thus recognized between theoretical theology and the practical rules of concern to the daily life and conduct of the individual. In the sphere of the applied sciences and the benefits they can bring to humanity, Islam maintains an open outlook. Thus it is not only acceptable but may even rank as *maṣlaḥah* (public interest) to employ scientific knowledge for the good of the people. Muslims have consequently not seen their faith as a hindrance to scientific knowledge. They have, on the contrary, made significant contributions to the advancement of science. The Prophet advocated beneficial knowledge (*al-ʿilm al-nāfiʿ*) that responds to people's legitimate needs, and accordingly instructed his followers to seek knowledge "even if it be in China." Thus it is not difficult to see that Islam accepts beneficial scientific knowledge from any source. China was certainly not known for religious knowledge, let alone Islamic, but was probably recognized then for its cultural attainments, scientific knowledge and wisdom.

The robust advocacy of *ʿilm* in the Qur'an, its open acceptance of knowledge gained through sense perception and observation, and its encouragement of enquiry and investigation of the world in which we live, all in all depict a basic alignment and convergence of interests between Islam and science, and not otherwise. Islamic philosophy that mainly studies purposes, as against science, which mainly studies causes, sees objects and events as signs (*āyāt*) of the Divine presence in the universe. Faith is understood by Muslims not as a limitation on science but as its vista for enrichment and perfection. Thinking Muslims should therefore work to vindicate the symbiotic relation of faith and reason, of knowledge and science, and advance a broader understanding of these and other civilisational objectives of Islam.

Consider, for instance, the use of stunning and the thoracic stick procedures, and whether they are acceptable from the Shariʿah viewpoint. Questions may arise as to how stunning and thoracic stick practices were originally introduced: for reasons of industry convenience, animal welfare, or both. Although the Shariʿah favours the smooth flow of lawful trade in the marketplace even at the expense of some compromise on other grounds, it does not favour measures that would present a threat to its higher values. Any decision that a Shariʿah specialist makes on stunning and thoracic stick issues, without the required scientific input, is bound to be based on externalities and assumptions that would be less than adequate – given the sensitivity of the issues and extensive application of the decisions in question. This also serves to illustrate the symbiotic relationship that we envisage between fiqh and scientific knowledge. Stunning and thoracic stick seem to have gained acceptance on the understanding that they help making slaughter relatively less painful for the animal. This is also in line with the Shariʿah principles. Malaysia's religious authorities have accepted the practice of stunning within a limited voltage range such that the sense perception of the animal is not completely obliterated. Electric stunning of larger animals like cows and sheep has been accepted in industrial slaughter practice in many Muslim countries. However, due to their smaller size, some had believed that chicken die from the shock that is supposed to stun them. Yet further investigation conducted in Turkey and the international Islamic Fiqh Academy seems to favour acceptance of stunning in chicken. The IIFA scholars who visited four plants in Turkey observed that in all the factories, chicken, before being slaughtered, were passed through electrified water for up to two seconds. The water with 40 ampses of current stuns the chicken. The IIFA scholars reported that some of the stunned chicken regained full consciousness in three minutes - hence the proof that they do not die of the current they were exposed to.[105]

The one area where Islam and science part ways is the rejection of metaphysical reality and the authority of revealed knowledge. Science is not receptive to these and Islam insists on its own articles of faith. One can, in sum, visualise compatibility in practical concerns of the benefits of science to humanity without however subscribing to its exclusively materialistic vision of reality and existence.

CONCLUSION AND RECOMMENDATIONS

Since the world Muslim community, or ummah is a unity in faith, its numerous component parts must remain open to learning from one another and appreciate their respective mores and cultural diversities within the wider unity of Islamic civilisation. If Islam can be characterised as diversity within unity, of sound *ikhtilāf* (disagreement) within the purview of *tawḥīd*, it is largely due to the unifying influence of the Qur'an, the exemplary teachings of the Prophet Muhammad, and a degree of consensus on basic values. The ummah also upholds a moral code of spiritual and legal dimensions that is grounded in the dual notions of *ḥalāl* and *ḥarām*. *Ḥalāl* food and *ḥalāl* trading and finance are among the tangible manifestations of the shared values that give the ummah its distinctive characteristics. Compared to *ikhtilāf*, *tawḥīd* is a much more prominent feature of Islam. Since uniformity and standardisation bear greater affinity with *tawḥīd*, to promote standardisation in the *ḥalāl* industry is not only desirable but also eminently feasible. The purpose of standardisation would naturally be better served if one aims at the common denominators of values, cultures and customs that can appeal to greater uniformity in trading practices as well as *ḥalāl* food and finance among Muslim countries and communities across the globe. Standardisation in all the material aspects of the *ḥalāl* industry should naturally take its cue from scriptural sources that constitute the basis of our efforts for uniformity and coordination throughout the Muslim world.

The fiqh discourse essentially elaborates and concretises the textual guidelines on *ḥalāl* and *ḥarām*, which also have devotional (*taʿabbudī*) features that go beyond common rationality. To promote uniformity in *ḥalāl* standards we propose the following:

- With regard to the *ḥalāl/mubāḥ*, and also the *makrūh* and the *mandūb*, greater uniformity and standardisation in the *ḥalāl* industry may be attempted by recourse to the principle of selection (*takhayyur*) and by singling out among the various rulings of the *madhāhib* ones that may be most suitable for that purpose. As an accepted method of Islamic jurisprudence, *takhayyur* is premised on the recognition that the leading schools of Islamic law have accepted one another as equally valid interpretations of the Shariʿah, which evidently offers potential for greater harmony and unification among them.

- Another method of selection we propose is the patching up (*talfīq*) of certain aspects of the rulings of different schools or jurists with a view to amalgamating them into unified formulas. *Talfīq* differs from *takhayyur* in that the latter selects the ruling as it is of a different *madhhab* to that of one's own, whereas *talfīq* attempts to combine certain parts of different rulings/interpretations into a single formula for the purpose of implementation.[106]
- To set up in every country and jurisdiction an authoritative Shariʿah advisory council that should ideally bring together a group of learned figures of standing from different disciplines. This should be sufficiently diversified so that its deliberations, advice and fatwa are informed by the scholastic thought of the various schools of thought, countries and cultural zones of the global ummah. The proposed council should also include representation from Muslim minorities in the West, as well as outstanding industry experts and market analysts.
- A set of procedural guidelines should be formulated to regulate the decision making and/or fatwa issuance by the Council. Plans should also be drawn up as to how the Council decisions could achieve high-level media impact and market penetration.
- Proactive measures should be taken for standardisation of *ḥalāl* practices by governments and industry participants both at macro and micro levels. One is reminded, in this connection, of an aspect of Islamic jurisprudence that authorises the ruling authorities (*'ūlī al-'amr*) to raise the *mandūb* into an obligatory command, or a *makrūh* into a prohibition, to regulate certain aspects of *mubāḥ*, and issue rulings on doubtful matters – if such

would be to the manifest *maṣlaḥah* of the people. The lawful authorities are thus empowered to introduce laws and formulate policies that secure the people's best interests in the light of prevailing circumstances. This function may be exercised by the elected legislature or a body of experts that works under its supervision.

- We also propose the creation of research institutes in Malaysia, the OIC headquarters and other Muslim countries that bring together researchers in Sharīʿah studies, food sciences, market specialists, and social scientists who can conduct research on market particularities, and the customs and cultures of the various countries and regions of the Islamic world. The Institute should act as the research arm of the Sharīʿah advisory council and make recommendations to the council on continuing developments in the *ḥalāl* industry and standardisation of *ḥalāl* procedures.
- Standardisation in the *ḥalāl* industry should also be informed by the approved mores and customs of Muslim communities. Since people's likes and dislikes in foodstuffs and marketing practices are influenced by a variety of factors, including climate, soil characteristics and even geographical proximity to other cultures, all of this may need to be taken into consideration in one's quest for promoting standardisation in the *ḥalāl* industry. These levels of diversity and variation are not always self-evident and may need to be verified and their Sharīʿah-compliance duly scrutinised through research. Hence we need to enrich our research efforts into the customary practices of countries and regions, as well as by setting in place consultative decision-making mechanisms that are duly informed by Sharīʿah, scientific and sociological research.
- Market researchers have consistently reported ambiguity and malpractice in the issuance and identification of *ḥalāl* logos and certifying authorities. This may be more extensive in non-Muslim majority countries, but the problem is much wider even in Muslim majority countries. In both cases the use of ambiguous and misleading words, phrases and signs have become problematic. As earlier mentioned the Malaysian authorities

were prompted into action by introducing as of January 2013, stiff fines for instances of violation that increase if repeated. This is a good approach but maybe a totally punitive approach is not the best; it should perhaps be supplemented by educational efforts and incentives for recognition of best performance awards to individual, producers and, suppliers as well as monitoring agencies of *ḥalāl* products and services.

NOTES

1. The reason why fiqh scholars opt for a different terminology may be due to the sensitivity that the Qur'an attaches to the pronouncement of the *ḥalāl* and *ḥarām*. For this is the prerogative only of God the Most High, as I shall elaborate. A slight difference in the meaning of these terms may also be relevant to note: whereas *mubāḥ* and *jā'iz* refer to something over which the Shari^cah is totally neutral, *ḥalāl* often implies a degree of purity in the context particularly of foodstuffs, and may as such imply preference that is not totally neutral.
2. The Arabic expressions used for *mubāḥ* are: *lā ithma, lā junāḥa, lā ba'sa, lā yu'ākhidhukum Allāh* etc.
3. The Arabic version is: *al-aṣlu fī al-ashyā' al-ibāḥah ḥattā yadullu al-dalīl ᶜalā al-taḥrīm*. Cf., Jalāl al-Dīn al-Suyūṭī, *al-Ashbāh wa al-Naẓā'ir* (Beirut: Dār al-Kutub al-ᶜIlmiyyah, 1983/1403 AH), p.60. A legal maxim normally consists of an abstract and epithetic statement of a fiqh position based on the overall reading of available evidence in the Qur'an and Hadith. By way of explanation, al-Suyūṭī raises the question as to the permissibility for human consumption, for instance, of giraffe saying that the jurists have not taken a position on this and it is therefore *ḥalāl* in the light of the said maxim and also the fact that giraffe is not a predatory animal.
4. Yusuf al-Qaradawi, *Al-Ḥalāl wa al-Ḥarām fī al-Islām* (Beirut: al-Maktab al-Islāmī, 1994/1415 AH, 15th ed.), 23; idem, *Bayᶜ al-Murābaḥah li al-Āmir bi al-Shirā'* (Cairo: Maktabah Wahbah, 1987/1407 AH, 2nd ed.), p.13. A sound (*ṣaḥīḥ*) hadith, as opposed to a weak one, is defined as a hadith with an unbroken *isnād* (chain of transmitters) all the way to the Prophet or a Companion, consisting of upright persons who possessed retentive memories and whose narration is not outlandish (*shādhdh*) and it is free of both obvious and subtle defects (*ᶜilal*). Cf., Mohammad Hashim Kamali, *A Textbook of Hadith Studies* (Leicester: The Islamic Foundation, 2005), p.139.

5. See for details, Wahbah al-Zuhayli, *Al-Fiqh al-Islāmī wa Adillatuh* (Damascus: Dār al-Fikr, 1989/1409 AH, 3rd ed.), 3:510f.
6. Cf., Mohammad Hashim Kamali, *Principles of Islamic Jurisprudence* (Cambridge: Islamic Texts Society, 2003), p. 429.
7. Ibid., 429.
8. Abū Isḥāq Ibrāhīm al-Shāṭibī, *Al-Muwāfaqāt fī Uṣūl al-Aḥkām*, ed. Muhammad Hasanayn Makhluf (Cairo: al-Maṭbaʿah al-Salafiyyah, 1920/1341 AH), 1:140f; Wahbah al-Zuhayli, *Uṣūl al-Fiqh al-Islāmī* (Damascus: Dār al-Fikr, 1986/1406 AH), p.86.
9. Cf., Yusuf al-Qaradawi, *Al-Ḥalāl wa al-Ḥarām*, p.31.
10. Al-Qaradawi, *Al-Ḥalāl wa al-Ḥarām*, p.56.
11. Certain *ṭayyibāt* were thus prohibited to the Jews as a matter however of reprimand and punishment (cf., Qur'an, *al-Anʿām*, 6:146 & *al-Nisā'*, 4:160).
12. In the case of liquor for example, the Qur'an explains its prohibition: "say that it is sinful but also benefits the people in some way, yet its evil is greater than its benefit." (*al-Baqarah*, 2:219). See also al-Qaradawi, *Al-Ḥalāl wa al-Ḥarām*, p.31.
13. The Arabic version reads "*idhā ijtamaʿ al-ḥalāl wa al-ḥarām, ghuliba al-ḥarām*". Jalāl al-Dīn al-Suyūṭī, *Al-Ashbāh wa al-Naḍā'ir* (Beirut: Dār al-Kutub al-ʿIlmiyyah, 1994), p.151. Shabir, *Al-Qawāʿid*, p.325. Interestingly enough, al-Qaradawi does not refer to this maxim in his brief discussion of "avoidance of the doubtful – *ittiqā' al-shubhāt*", which is perhaps not accidental, due to some weakness in its evidential basis and also another line of evidence that advises taking that which is the easier course and brings facility and relief. This may also explain why al-Qaradawi subsumes the issue under the rubric of *sadd al-dharā'iʿ*.
14. See for a discussion, Securities Commission, Resolutions of the Securities Commission Shariah Advisory Council, 2nd ed. Kuala Lumpur, 2007, p.158.
15. The legal maxim in Arabic reads: "*Dar' al-mafāsid awlā min jalb al-manāfiʿ*."
16. Cf., Shabir, *Al-Qawāʿid*, pp. 326–8.
17. Wizārat al-Awqāf wa al-Shu'ūn al-Islāmiyyah, *Al-Mawsūʿah al-Fiqhiyyah* (Kuwait: Wizārat al-Awqāf wa al-Shu'ūn al-Islāmiyyah, 1421 AH/2001), 40:75.
18. Ibid.
19. Ibid., 40:79 and 85.

20. The ten items include pork, blood, dead carcasses, animals that had been strangled, beaten, fallen, gored, that which had been partly eaten by wild beasts, and animals slaughtered in the name of deities other than Allah, and that which is sacrificed on stone (altars).
21. Cf., Umar Sulayman al-Ashqar, Muhammad Uthman Shabir et al., *Dirāsāt Fiqhiyyah fī Qaḍāyā Ṭibbiyyah al-Muᶜāṣirah* (Amman: Dār al-Nafā'is, 1421 AH/2001), p.317.
22. Muslim jurists are thus unanimous on the filth of human excrements and excrements of carnivorous animals and also on their urine, although on the latter with some differences of opinion. They have differed more widely on the excrements and urine of 'slaughterable' animals, non-carnivorous animals, and birds.
23. Cf., Ahmad al-Hajji al-Kurdi, *Buḥūth wa Fatāwā Fiqhiyyah Muᶜāṣirah* (Beirut: Dār al-Bashā'ir al-Islāmiyyah, 1427 AH/2007), pp.29-31.
24. Ibid., p.313.
25. Wizārat al-Awqāf wa al-Shu'ūn al-Islāmiyyah, *Al-Mawsūᶜah*, 40:74 and 77; see also 40:101-103.
26. Al-Ashqar et al., *Dirāsāt*, p.318.
27. Ibid., p.314.
28. Ibid., p.317.
29. Cf., Yusuf al-Qaradawi, *Al-Ḥalāl wa al-Ḥarām*, p.15; Muhammad Uthman Shabir, *Al-Qawāᶜid al-Kulliyyah wa al-Ḍawābiṭ al-Fiqhiyyah fī al-Shariᶜah al-Islāmiyyah* (Amman: Dār al-Nafā'is, 2006/1426 AH), p.324; Kamali, *Principles*, p.421.
30. The Qur'anic prohibition of pig meat represents a continuation of the Judaic tradition. Similarly the negative view of the Islamic tradition toward dogs is attributed to the fact that the canines were often seen as carriers of rabies and best kept at a safe distance.
31. Ibn Mājah al-Qazwīnī, ed. Muammad Fuad Abd al-Baqi, *Sunan Ibn Mājah* (Beirut: Dār al-Kutub al-ᶜIlmiyyah, 1987/1407 AH), ḥadīth no. 3,367; al-Qaradawi, *Al-Ḥalāl wa al-Ḥarām*, p.23.
32. See for details on *siyāsah sharᶜiyyah*, Mohammad Hashim Kamali, *Shariᶜah Law: An Introduction* (Oxford: Oneworld Publications, 2008), pp.225-245.
33. Cf., Al-Qaradawi, *Al-Ḥalāl wa al-Ḥarām*, p.34; Shabir, *Al-Qawāᶜid*, p.324.
34. Cf., Al-Qaradawi, *Al-Ḥalāl wa al-Ḥarām*, pp.37-8. Minor exceptions exist

here in the case, for instance, of *ribā* (usury) that a Muslim may practise, in relationship to a non-Muslim. But this too, is a disputed opinion and some jurists consider it invalid, while others say that only if the non-Muslim is a *rābī* and resident of a hostile country.

35. Ibid., p.34. Al-Qaradawi illustrates this by say calling casino dance as a form of art, or *ribā* as profit.
36. Cf. Wizārat al-Awqāf wa al-Shu'ūn al-Islāmiyyah, al-Mawsūʿah al-Fiqhiyyah (Kuwait, 1993/1414 AH, 4th ed.), 5:125.
37. Ibid.
38. Muslim, *Mukhtaṣar Ṣaḥīḥ Muslim*, ed. Muhammad Nasir al-Din al-Albani (Beirut: Dār al-Maktab al-Islāmī, 1987), p.342, hadih no. 1,262.
39. ʿAlā' al-Dīn al-Kāsānī, *Badā'iʿ al-Ṣanā'iʿ fī tartīb al-sharā'iʿ* (Beirut: Dār al-Kutub al-ʿIlmiyyah, 1986/1406 AH), 2nd ed., 5:114; al-Zuhayli, *Al-Fiqh al-Islāmī*, 3:5.
40. The substance of this is also conveyed in a hadith: "It is forbidden to take the property of a Muslim without his consent." See Abū Bakr ʿAbd al-Raḥmān ibn al-Ḥusayn al-Bayhaqī, *Al-Sunan al-Kubrā*, ed. M. Abd al-Qadir Ata (Mecca: Maktabah Dār al-Bāz, 1987/1407 AH), 6:100, hadith no. 11,325. We also read in another hadith: "You and your property both belong to your father." See Muḥammad ibn ʿAbd Allāh al-Khaṭīb al-Tabrīzī, *Mishkāt al-Maṣābīḥ*, ed. Muhammad Nasir al-Din al-Albani (Beirut: Dār al-Maktab al-Islāmī, 1979/1399), 2nd ed., hadith no. 3,354.
41. Muhammad Uthman Shabir, *Al-Qawāʿid al-Kulliyyah wa al-Ḍawābiṭ al-Fiqhiyyah* (Amman: Dār al-Nafā'is, 1426 AH/2006), p.213.
42. Cf. Wahbah al-Zuhaili, *Al-Fiqh al-Islāmī*, vol. 6, p.161f.
43. ʿAlā' al-Dīn al-Kāsānī, *Badā'iʿ al-Ṣanā'iʿ fī Tartīb al-Sharā'iʿ* (Beirut: Dār al-Kutub al-ʿIlmiyyah, 1986/1406 AH), 5:113, claims a conclusive consensus (ijmaʿ) on the prohibition of even a smallest quantity of alcohol. See for a discussion of *sadd al-dharā'iʿ*, Kamali, *Jurisprudence*, chapter 16, pp.397–410.
44. Cf. Wahbbah al-Zuhayli, *Al-Fiqh al-Islāmī*, vol. 6, p.166.
45. Cf., Abdul Rahman Awang, "Istihalah and the Sunnah of the Prophet," in: Halal Development Corporation, *The Essence of Halal*, p.58.
46. Ibid. See also on *istiḥālah*, Ahmad al-Hajji al-Kurdi, *Buḥūth wa Fatāwā Fiqhiyyah Muʿāṣirah* (Beirut: Dār al-Bashā'ir al-Islāmiyyah, 1427 AH/2007), p.29.

47. http:www.islamset.org/bioethics/9thfiqh.html#1 (accessed on 10 January 2012).
48. The Fiqh Academy decision was carried in *al-Sharq al-Awsat* (London), no. 9173, 9 July 2004, p.14, available online at http://www.asharqalawsat.com/print.asp?did=211692 (accessed on 10 January 2012).
49. http://www.islamset.org/bioethics/8thfiq.html (accessed on 10 January 2012).
50. Nazih Hammad, "Dieting the Islamic Way," available online at http://www. themodernreligion.com/health/diet.html (accessed on 10 January 2012); also quoted by Abdul Rahman Awang, "*Istiḥālah*," p.60.
51. http://www.islamset.org/bioethics/8fiqh.html (accessed on 10 January 2012).
52. See for details Muhammad Abu Zahrah, *Uṣūl al-Fiqh* (Cairo: Dār al-Fikr al-ʿArabī, 1958/1366 AH), p.34; Kamali, *Principles*, p.424.
53. Cf., Kamali, *Principles*, p.426.
54. Thus according to one hadith "The Prophet proscribed eating the flesh of a *jallalah* camel," and according to another "The Prophet proscribed drinking the milk of a *jallalah*." Both hadiths are quoted in *Sunan Dāraquṭnī* and *Sunan Abū Dāwūd*, respectively, and quoted in Wizārat al-Awqāf wa al-Shu'ūn al-Islāmiyyah, *Al-Mawsūʿah al-fiqhiyyah*, 5:149.
55. Al-Kāsānī, *Badā'iʿ*, 5:39–40; Muhammad Amin ibn Abidin, *Hāshiyah Radd al-Mukhtār ʿalā Durr al-Mukhtār* (Cairo: Dār al-Fikr, 1979/1300 AH), 5:194.
56. Abū Ḥafṣ ʿUmar ibn Badr al-Mawṣillī, *Al-Jamʿu Bayn al-Ṣaḥīḥayn* (Beirut: al-Maktab al-Islāmī, 1995), vol.2, p.38.
57. Al-Shāṭibī, *Al-Muwāfaqāt*, p.152
58. Cf., Al-Zuhayli, *Al-Fiqh al-Islāmī*, 3:667.
59. Cf., Wizārat al-Awqāf wa al-Shu'ūn al-Islāmiyyah, *Al-Mawsūʿah al-Fiqhiyyah*, 5:152.
60. Ibid., 5:153.
61. Ibid., 5:155.
62. Cf., Ibn Rushd, *Bidāyat al-Mujtahid* (Beirut: Dār al-Qalam, 1988), 1:329; al-Zuhayli, *Al-Fiqh al-Islāmī*, 3:663–4.
63. Susan Douglas, "The Fabric of Muslim Daily Life," in ed. Vincent Cornell, *Voices of Islam* (Praeger: Connecticut, 2007), vol. 3, p.17.
64. See for details, Kamali, *Principles*, p.331.

65. Muhammad A. al-Bayanuni, *Al-Ḥukm al-Taklīfiī fī al-Sharīʿah al-Islāmiyyah* (Damascus: Dār al-Qalam, 1988), pp.224-225.
66. Ibid, p.225
67. See for details Kamali, *Principles*, p.419f.
68. The hadith reports also mention a special variety of dates, known as *ʿajwah*, that the Prophet liked most and spoke well of its nutritional value. See for details of hadith reports on this and other food items, Abdul Rahman Awang, "*Istiḥālah* and the Sunnah of the Prophet," in Halal Industry Development Corporation, *The Essence of Halal* (Kuala Lumpur: HDC Publication, 2011), pp.72-73, also www.mdcpublishers.com.
69. Hadith reported by al-Bukhārī on the authority of Abū Umaymah, quoted in Ibid., p.70.
70. See for details, Ibid., pp.70-71.
71. Muslim, *Mukhtaṣar Ṣaḥīḥ Muslim*, p. 253, hadith no. 956.
72. Al-Qaradawi, *Al-Ḥalāl wa al-Ḥarām*, p.37.
73. Al-Tabrīzī, *Mishkāt*, 2:845, hadith no. 4,046.
74. BSE stands for bovine spongiform encephalopathy. See more on this in Richard C. Foltz, *Animals in Islamic Tradition and Muslim Countries* (Oxford: Oneworld Publications, 2006), p.118. Foltz thus informs us on the same page that "Middle Eastern countries now import much of their meat from places such as New Zealand and that factory farming presents considerable difficulties in verifying whether meat is *ḥalāl*."
75. The Arabic version reads "*idhā ijtamaʿ al-ḥalāl wa al-ḥarām, ghuliba al-ḥarām.*" Jalāl al-Dīn al-Suyūṭī, *Al-Ashbāh wa al-Naẓā'ir* (Beirut: Dār al-Kitāb al-ʿIlmiyyah, 1994), p.151. Shabir, *Al-Qawāʿid*, p.325. Interestingly enough, al-Qaradawi does not refer to this maxim in his brief discussion of "avoidance of the doubtful – *ittiqā' al-shubuhāt*," which is perhaps not accidental, due to some weakness in its evidential basis and also another line of evidence that advises taking that which is the easier course and brings facility and relief. This may also explain why al-Qaradawi subsumes the issue under the rubric of *sadd al-dharā'iʿ*.
76. See for a discussion, Securities Commission, Resolutions of the Securities Commission Shariah Advisory Council, 2nd ed., Kuala Lumpur, 2007, p.158.
77. The legal maxim in Arabic reads: "*Dar' al-mafāsid awlā min jalb al-manāfiʿ*."
78. Cf., Shabir, *Al-Qawāʿid*, pp.326–8.

79. Cf., Mohammad Hashim Kamali, "The Principles of Halal and Haram in Islam," in ed. Halal Development Corporation, *The Modern Compendium of Halal*, vol. 1, *The Essence of Halal* (Kuala Lumpur, 2011), p.24f.
80. Cf. Kamali, "Principles of Halal and Haram," in ed. Halal Development Corporation, *The Essence of Halal*, p.38f.
81. Cf., Qur'an, *Al-Naḥl*, 16:115. See also Susan L. Douglas, "The Fabric of Muslim Daily Life," in ed. Vincent Cornell, *Voices of Islam* (Westport, Connecticut), vol. 3, pp.16-17.
82. Cf. Kamali, "Principles of Halal and Haram," in ed. Halal Development Corporation, *The Essence of Halal*, p.42f.
83. Al-Qaradawi, *Al-Ḥalal wa al-Ḥarām*, p.63.
84. See report by Nurbaiti Hamdan and A Raman. *The Star*, 11 September 2008, p. N43.
85. Report in New Straits Times of Kuala Lumpur, December 29, 2012, p.10.
86. Marco Tieman, "Control of Halal Food Chains," *Islam and Civilisational Renewal* (Kuala Lumpur), 3.3, 2011, pp.538–542.
87. Al-Qaradawi, *Al-Ḥalāl wa al-Ḥarām*, p.72.
88. Al-Qaradawi, *Al-Ḥalāl wa al-Ḥarām*, p.53; Abdul Halim Uwais, *Mawsūʿah al-Fiqh al-Islāmī* (Egypt: Dār al-Wafā'), vol.1, p.174.
89. Foltz, *Animals*, p.27.
90. See for details al-Qaradawi, *Al-Ḥalāl wa al-Ḥarām*, p.61; al-Zuhayli, *Al-Fiqh al-Islāmī*, 3:659.
91. Al-Qaradawi, *Al-Ḥalāl wa al-Ḥarām*, pp.61–2.
92. Ibn Rushd, *Bidāyat al-Mujtahid*, 1:325f; al-Zuhayli, *Al-Fiqh al-Islāmī*, 3:661–3.
93. Ibn Rushd, *Bidāyat al-Mujtahid*, 1:327–8; al-Zuhayli, *Al-Fiqh al-Islāmī*, 3:663–4; al-Qaradawi, *Al-Ḥalāl wa al-Ḥarām*, 55f.
94. Abū Dāwūd, *Sunan Abū Dāwūd*, Engl. tr. Ahmad Hassan (Lahore: Sh. Ashraf, 1984), 2:1149, hadith no. 411. See for a discussion also, Kamali, *Principles*, p.153.
95. Al-Qaradawi, *Al-Ḥalāl wa al-Ḥarām*, pp.51–2.
96. Ibid., p.51.
97. Cf., Kamali, *Principles*, 369; Shabir, *Al-Qawāʿid*, p.244 f.
98. *The Mejelle*, being an English translation of *Majallah el-Ahkam-i Adliya and A Complete Code of Islamic Civil Law*, tr. C.R. Tyser et al. (Kuala Lumpur: The Other Press, 2003, repr.), Art. 36. *The Mejelle* records several other legal

maxims on custom, including "the use of men is evidence according to which it is necessary to act" (Art. 37). See for further details Kamali, *Principles*, p. 371.

99. Shahidan Shafie and Mohd Nor Othman, "Halal Certification: International Marketing Issues and Challenges," Kuala Lumpur, Faculty of Business and Accountancy, University of Malaya, unpublished conference paper, p.2.
100. Roziana Hamsawi, "Bumis only Hold 30pc of Halal Certs," *New Straits Times* (Kuala Lumpur), 29 June 2011, p.5.
101. Ibid.
102. See for details Sabariyah Din, *Trading Halal Commodities: Opportunities and Challenges for the Muslim World* (Kuala Lumpur: Penerbit Universiti Teknologi Malaysia, 2006), pp.20-21.
103. Roziana Hamsawi, "Bumis."
104. Shahidan Shafie and Mohd Nor Othman, "Halal Certification," p.5.
105. http://www.upc-online.org/slaughter /report/html.
106. See for details on *takhayyur* and *talfīq*, Mohammad Hashim Kamali, "Shariʿah and Civil Law: Toward a Methodology of Harmonisation," *Islamic Law and Society* 14 (2007), pp.406–11.